VOTES
FOR
WOMEN

Women Making History:
The 19th Amendment

National Park Service
U.S. Department of the Interior

Edited by Tamara Gaskell

Table of Contents

Preface

Since its inception in 1916, the National Park Service (NPS) has been dedicated to the preservation and management of the United States' outstanding natural, historical, and recreational resources. The NPS cares for special places that are the heritage of all Americans, and manages programs that support communities around the United States and its territories with preserving their historic places and sharing their own important local history.

The NPS is excited to commemorate the 100th year anniversary of the passage of the Nineteenth Amendment to the US Constitution that abolished sex as a basis for voting, and to tell the diverse history of women's suffrage—the right to vote—more broadly. The US Congress passed the Nineteenth Amendment on June 4, 1919 and the states ratified the amendment on August 18, 1920, officially recognizing women's right to vote. NPS encourages visitors to connect with the historic places around the country where this pivotal national story occurred.

The following handbook demonstrates the expansiveness of the stories that NPS is telling to preserve and protect women's history for this and future generations. The struggle to secure women's suffrage is an international story—one started well before the Nineteenth Amendment passed. And truthfully, issues of voting rights and who has access are debated to this current day. From historical actors that opposed women's suffrage to the struggle by African American women—sometimes violently suppressed—to exercise their voting rights to the legal and social restrictions that remained against other women of color post-passage, the essays tell a broad history of various women advocating for their rights. The NPS champions the importance of interpretation and education that makes visible all peoples and their communities in the women's suffrage story and in America's national parks and historic preservation programs.

Thank you for joining the Nation and NPS on this important journey,

Dr. Turkiya L. Lowe, NPS Chief Historian
Washington, DC

Note to readers: endnotes and sources for these essays are online at www.nps.gov/articles/19th-amendment-in-america-bibliography.htm

Explore more of the NPS commemoration of the Nineteenth Amendment Centennial at www.nps.gov/womenshistory

1756

October 30: Lydia Taft, recent widow of Josiah Taft, of Uxbridge, Massachusetts, is allowed to vote as Josiah's proxy at a town meeting. The vote was regarding the town's involvement in the French and Indian Wars. Lydia is the first white woman to vote in what was to become the United States. (Women in many communities who lived here before Europeans arrived were leaders and influenced decisions).

Independence Hall in Philadelphia, ca. 2010.

Women and men in early America. Women played important roles in colonial society, yet they were often prohibited from participating in civic life.

1787

May to September: The United States Constitutional Convention is held at what is now Independence Hall in Philadelphia. At the convention, it is decided that states have the right to determine qualifications required to vote.

Signing of the United States Constitution at the Constitutional Convention of 1787.

1790

March 26: The Naturalization Act of 1790 passes. It allows white men born outside of the United States to become citizens. Because the ability to decide voting requirements is held by the states, becoming a citizen does not automatically confer voting rights.

The Assembly Room of Independence Hall. The US government met here until Washington, DC became the official meeting space of the new government.

1848

July 19-20: The first Women's Rights Convention in the US is held in Seneca Falls, New York. Three hundred attend the convention organized in part by Elizabeth Cady Stanton. Frederick Douglass is one of those present. One hundred of the attendees sign the Declaration of Sentiments, which includes a call for women's access to the vote.

1850

October 23-24: The First National Women's Rights Convention is held in Worcester, Massachusetts. Almost 1,000 men and women from eleven states (including California) attend.

1857

March: The US Supreme Court rules in *Dred Scott v. Sandford* that the US Constitution is not meant to include Black people as citizens. The Dred Scott decision is later overturned by the Thirteenth Amendment to the US Constitution (abolishing slavery) and the Fourteenth Amendment to the US Constitution (conferring citizenship on all persons born or naturalized in the United States).

Dred and Harriet Scott, ca. 1887.

1868

July 9: The Fourteenth Amendment is adopted. It defines who is a citizen of the United States: "All persons born or naturalized in the United States, and subject to the jurisdiction thereof, are citizens of the United States and of the State wherein they reside." Women, therefore, are citizens (unless part of a group excluded from this amendment). After this, questions of what rights and responsibilities come with citizenship are debated.

1869

May 12: The American Equal Rights Association, originally formed in 1866, undergoes a painful split at their annual meeting. Attendees include Frederick Douglass, Lucy Stone, Elizabeth Cady Stanton, and Susan B. Anthony. At the meeting, Frederick Douglass argues that Black men's right to vote should take precedence over women's right to vote, "With us, the matter is a question of life and death." Anthony replies that, despite that, Douglass "would not exchange his sex." Lucy Stone states that "woman suffrage is more imperative than his own."

May 15: The National Woman Suffrage Association (NWSA) is established by Elizabeth Cady Stanton, Susan B. Anthony, and others.

November: The American Woman Suffrage Association (AWSA) is founded, led by Lucy Stone. The group is made up largely of members of the New England Woman Suffrage Association.

December 10: Women in Wyoming Territory are granted unrestricted suffrage.

1870

March 30: The Fifteenth Amendment becomes law. It prohibits exclusion from voting "on account of race, color, or previous condition of servitude." In response, many former Confederate states pass Jim Crow laws that disenfranchise Black and poor white men from voting through poll taxes, literacy tests, and other restrictions.

1871

January 11: Victoria Woodhull testifies to the Judiciary Committee of the United States House of Representatives (the first woman to address a House committee). She argues that the Fourteenth Amendment grants women the right to vote. The committee disagrees.

1872

November 5: Susan B. Anthony is one of several women in Rochester, New York to vote in the presidential election. Anthony is arrested and charged with voting illegally. Her case is heard by a federal court, who issue their decision in 1873. The other women who voted are arrested but not charged. The election inspectors who allowed the women to vote are arrested and found guilty. President Ulysses S. Grant pardons them after they are jailed for refusing to pay their fines.

1873

June: In *United States v. Susan B. Anthony*, the court concludes that citizenship does not automatically confer the right to vote. Susan B. Anthony is convicted of voting without having the right to do so. She is fined $100 for voting; she never pays. Because the judge rules that Anthony will not be jailed for failure to pay, her case cannot move to the US Supreme Court.

Susan B. Anthony

Victoria Woodhull testifying in front of Judiciary Committee of the House of Representatives, 1871.

Virginia Minor, ca. 1850-1893.

1875

March 29: The US Supreme Court decides Virginia Minor's case. She argues that Missouri's limiting of the vote to men is unconstitutional. While the court agrees that women are citizens and therefore "entitled to all the privileges and immunities of citizenship," voting is not one of them. "The Constitution," they write, "does not confer the right of suffrage upon any one."

1880

Mary Ann Shadd Cary establishes the Colored Women's Franchise Association in Washington, DC. The organization links suffrage to political rights as well as education and labor issues.

1884

November 3: The United States Supreme Court decides in *Elk v. Wilkins* that Native Americans are not eligible to vote in US elections, even if they own property and pay taxes. Their logic is that they are citizens of Indian nations, not of the United States – even if, like John Elk, they have given up their tribal affiliation and culture.

Late 1880s

Sarah Garnet establishes the Brooklyn Colored Woman's Equal Suffrage League, the first organization of Black women devoted solely to suffrage.

1887

February 8: The Dawes Act grants US citizenship to Native Americans, but only those willing to give up their tribal membership, lands, and culture. Despite being citizens, Native Americans are still considered "wards" of the federal government, and therefore generally forbidden to vote in US local, state, or federal elections.

1890

February 18: The National Woman Suffrage Association and the American Woman Suffrage Association merge to form the National American Woman Suffrage Association.

July 10: Wyoming becomes a state. With woman suffrage included in its new state constitution, Wyoming becomes the first state with woman suffrage.

1893

Colorado state voters pass woman suffrage with 55% of the vote.

1895

July: The National Conference of the Colored Women of America convenes, organized by Josephine St. Pierre Ruffin and the Woman's Era Club. From this meeting comes the Federation of African-American Women, the forerunner of the National Association of Colored Women (founded in 1896). These groups focus in part on woman suffrage, as well as other issues affecting Black women.

1896

January 4: Utah becomes a state. Woman suffrage is included in the new state constitution.

July: The National Association of Colored Women is founded. Members advocate for woman suffrage and women's rights.

1898

August 12: The Territory of Hawai'i is established. Woman suffrage is explicitly left out of the

National American Woman Suffrage Association Headquarters, ca. 1913.

Queen Lili'uokalani, ca. 1891

territorial constitution. The last indigenous ruler of the islands, Queen Lili'uokalani, is removed from power by the United States in 1893.

1908

February 16: Members of New York City's Women's Progressive Suffrage Union march from Union Square to the Manhattan Trade School. Denied a permit and despite police attempts to break them up, the Suffrage Union finishes their march. This is the first suffrage march in the United States.

1909

February 12: The National Association for the Advancement of Colored People (NAACP) is established in New York City by white and Black members. The NAACP became an important organization in the fight for suffrage, both for women and for Black men in the South.

1911

March 25: The Triangle Shirtwaist Fire in New York City results in the deaths of 145 workers. The tragedy spurs increased collaboration between working women and middle-class reformers, who advocate for woman suffrage as a way to change working conditions.

October 10: California voters approve a woman suffrage measure on the state ballot. Women win the vote across the state with 50.7 percent of the vote.

1912

May 19: Tye Leung Shulze of California becomes the first Chinese person in America to vote.

November 18: Oregon citizens vote in a woman suffrage referendum. The referendum passes with 52% in favor.

Kansas grants women full suffrage as part of a state constitutional amendment recognizing universal suffrage.

1913

January 30: Ida B. Wells-Barnett establishes the Alpha Suffrage Club, the first Black women's suffrage organization in Illinois.

Ida B. Wells

March: The Alaska Territorial Legislature passes woman suffrage as its first order of business following the establishment of the Alaska Territory. It grants the vote "to such women as have the qualifications of citizenship required of male electors." It excludes Alaska Natives.

March 3: The Woman Suffrage Procession, organized by Alice Paul and The Congressional Union, marches through the streets of Washington, DC on the eve of Woodrow Wilson's presidential inauguration. The parade, the largest yet held, draws as many as half a million people to watch. Paraders are attacked by mobs; Boy Scouts provide some protection and first aid to some of the hundreds of women who are injured. No arrests are made.

June 26: Illinois grants women the vote in presidential elections.

1914

November 3: Montana grants women the vote via referendum, with a 52.2 percent majority.

1915

The Alaska Territorial Legislature recognizes the right of Indigenous people to vote, on the condition they give up their tribal customs and traditions.

1916

June 5: Alice Paul and the Congressional Union break completely with the National American Woman Suffrage Association and form the National Woman's Party.

Suffragists Picket the White House, ca. 1917

November: Jeannette Rankin is elected to represent Montana in the US House of Representatives. She is the first woman elected to US Congress. She takes office in March 1917.

1917

January: The National Woman's Party organizes "Silent Sentinel" pickets outside the White House, the first time the White House is picketed by protesters. The pickets continue through early 1919.

May 8: Michigan woman gain access to the vote for US President.

June: Police begin arresting Silent Sentinels. Over the next two years, more than 500 women are arrested and 168 of them incarcerated. Many of those jailed at Occoquan Workhouse in Virginia go on hunger strikes, and are force-fed.

November: Oklahoma voters approve a woman suffrage amendment to the state constitution. The amendment passes easily.

November 6: New York voters approve a woman suffrage amendment to the state constitution, with 59% voting for it.

November 14: The "Night of Terror" at the Occoquan Workhouse. Jailed "Silent Sentinels" are beaten, chained in stress positions, and rendered unconscious.

November 27-28: All Silent Sentinels are released from prison after public outrage over their treatment.

Rhode Island opens presidential voting to women.

1918

January 9: President Woodrow Wilson gives a speech promoting the United States as a beacon of democracy. He urges Congress to support woman suffrage as a war measure.

November 5: South Dakota voters approve full woman suffrage in a state-wide referendum. The vote was 63% for; 37% against.

Michigan voters approve a state constitutional amendment granting women full suffrage.

1919

May 21: The US House of Representatives passes the 19th Amendment legislation.

June 4: The US Senate votes to pass the 19th Amendment legislation—The race to ratification begins!

June 10: Michigan, Wisconsin— The first states to ratify the 19th Amendment.

June 16: Kansas, New York, Ohio ratify the 19th Amendment.

June 17: Illinois voted on June 10 in favor of the 19th Amendment, but ratification was not finalized until June 17.

June 24: Pennsylvania ratifies the 19th Amendment.

June 25: Massachusetts ratifies the 19th Amendment.

June 28: Texas ratifies the 19th Amendment.

July 2: Iowa ratifies the 19th Amendment.

July 3: Missouri ratifies the 19th Amendment.

July 24: Georgia votes to reject the 19th Amendment.

July 28: Arkansas ratifies the 19th Amendment.

August 2: Montana, Nebraska ratify the 19th Amendment.

September 8: Minnesota ratifies the 19th Amendment.

September 10: New Hampshire ratifies the 19th Amendment.

Jeannette Rankin, ca. 1917

September 22: Alabama votes to reject the 19th Amendment.

October 2: Utah ratifies the 19th Amendment.

November 1: California ratifies the 19th Amendment.

November 5: Maine ratifies the 19th Amendment.

December 1: North Dakota ratifies the 19th Amendment.

December 4: South Dakota ratifies the 19th Amendment.

December 15: Colorado ratifies the 19th Amendment.

1920

January 6: Kentucky, Rhode Island ratify the 19th Amendment.

January 13: Oregon ratifies the 19th Amendment.

January 16: Indiana ratifies the 19th Amendment.

January 27: Wyoming ratifies the 19th Amendment.

January 28: South Carolina votes to reject the 19th Amendment.

February 7: Nevada ratifies the 19th Amendment.

February 9: New Jersey ratifies the 19th Amendment.

February 11: Idaho ratifies the 19th Amendment.

February 12: Arizona votes to ratify the 19th Amendment while Virginia votes to reject it.

February 21: New Mexico ratifies the 19th Amendment.

February 24: Maryland votes to reject the 19th Amendment.

February 28: Oklahoma ratifies the 19th Amendment.

March 10: West Virginia ratifies the 19th Amendment.

March 22: Washington ratifies the 19th Amendment.

March 29: Mississippi votes to reject the 19th Amendment.

June 2: Delaware senate votes in favor of the 19th Amendment (11 to 6), but the state house refuses to vote on the measure, killing it.

July 1: Louisiana votes to reject the 19th Amendment.

August 18: Tennessee becomes the 36th state to ratify the 19th Amendment.

August 26: Certified into law by the US Secretary of State as the 19th Amendment to the US Constitution.

September 14: Connecticut ratifies the 19th Amendment.

1921

February 8: Vermont ratifies the 19th Amendment.

September 24: The National Woman's Party begins to campaign for what becomes known as the Equal Rights Amendment. Several revisions to the text are made, but the one that reaches Congress reads, in part, "Equality of rights under the law shall not be denied or abridged by the United States or by any State on account of sex."

1923

March 6: Delaware ratifies the 19th Amendment.

1924

June 24: The US Congress passes the Indian Citizenship Act, defining Native Americans as US citizens. The Bureau of Indian Affairs sends guidance to their staff across the country clarifying that citizenship does not necessarily include the right to vote. Many states continue to disenfranchise indigenous people; some states responded to the Act by passing laws designed to keep Native Americans from the vote.

1929

Literate women in Puerto Rico are granted the vote.

1935

All women in Puerto Rico are granted suffrage.

1937

December 6: In *Breedlove v. Suttles*, the US Supreme Court concludes that poll taxes set by states are constitutional. Poll taxes are used to prevent people with little money (i.e. poor whites, African Americans, Native Americans) from voting.

1941

March 29: Maryland ratifies the 19th Amendment, but the vote is not certified until February 25, 1958.

1943

December 17: The Magnuson Act becomes federal law. It repeals the 1882 Chinese Exclusion Act, and Chinese immigrants, including women, are able to become US citizens (though rights of property ownership remain restricted). Some already in the US are able to naturalize. The quota for entry visas to the US issued to Chinese citizens is set at 105 per year.

1952

February 21: Virginia ratifies the 19th Amendment.

1953

September 8: Alabama ratifies the 19th Amendment.

1958

Maryland certifies their 1941 19th Amendment ratification vote.

Exterior of the Belmont-Paul Women's Equality National Monument in Washington, DC

1961

April 3: The 23rd Amendment to the US Constitution becomes law. It grants residents of Washington, DC the right to vote for US President. Because DC is not a state, residents do not have voting representatives in the US Congress.

1964

January 23: The 24th Amendment to the US Constitution is ratified. It formally abolishes poll taxes and literacy tests as barriers to voting.

1965

August 6: President Johnson signs the Voting Rights Act into law. It prohibits racial discrimination in voting. Later amendments to the Act expand its protections.

1968

April 11: The Civil Rights Act of 1968 becomes law. It prescribes penalties for certain acts of violence or intimidation in certain circumstances. This includes interfering with a person's access to the vote.

1969

May 13: Florida ratifies the 19th Amendment.

July 1: South Carolina ratifies the 19th Amendment; the vote is not certified until August 22, 1973.

1970

February 20: Georgia ratifies the 19th Amendment.

June 11: Louisiana ratifies the 19th Amendment.

August 10: The Equal Rights Amendment, originally drafted by Alice Paul in the 1920s, passes the United States House of Representatives. It is not brought to a vote in the US Senate.

1971

May 6: North Carolina ratifies the 19th Amendment.

July 5: The 26th Amendment to the US Constitution is signed into law. It prohibits states and the federal government from preventing US citizens who are at least 18 years old from voting based on their age.

1972

March 22: The Equal Rights Amendment passes in the US Senate with a vote of 84 for, 8 against. The Equal Rights Amendment goes to the states for ratification. Thirty-eight states are required to ratify the Amendment for it to become law.

The Sewall-Belmont House becomes an affiliated unit of the National Park Service as the Sewall-Belmont National Historic Site. The National Woman's Party has had their headquarters in this Washington, DC building since 1929.

1973

August 22: South Carolina certifies their 19th Amendment ratification vote of July 1, 1969.

1980

December 28: Women's Rights National Historical Park is established. It includes several properties associated with the 1848 Women's Rights convention in Seneca Falls. It is a unit of the National Park Service.

1984

Mississippi ratifies the 19th Amendment.

2016

The Sewall-Belmont National Historic Site is designated a National Monument. It is incorporated into the National Park Service as Belmont-Paul Women's Equality National Monument.

2020

January 15: Virginia is the 38th state to ratify the Equal Rights Amendment. Other legal factors are in play, and the fate of the ERA remains undecided.

—Megan E. Springate

Interior of Belmont-Paul Women's Equality National Monument. Bust of Susan B. Anthony (left) and Alva Belmont, and statue of Joan of Arc (far right) in front hallway.

Looking for a Right to Vote: Introducing the Nineteenth Amendment

by Ann D. Gordon

The year 2020 marks a significant centennial: ratification of a federal constitutional amendment that barred states from excluding women from the electorate solely on the basis of their sex. We pay tribute to the tens of thousands of women who envisaged a government in which men and women had equal voice and who, through agitation and persistent mobilization of citizens, brought about that change. This was a long fight. Historians point to different moments of origin, but their choices fall into the 1830s and 1840s. If dated from the women's rights convention at Seneca Falls, New York, in 1848, seventy-two years passed before ratification of the federal amendment—and that's the short version.

As we celebrate, it matters that we not overstate the changes wrought by the Nineteenth Amendment. *It does not confer voting rights on anyone.* This is its pith:

> *Section 1. The right of citizens of the United States to vote shall not be denied or abridged by the United States or by any state on account of sex.*

Advocates of woman suffrage adopted the model created by Congress to extend voting rights to freedmen after the Civil War in the Fifteenth Amendment of 1870. In that case the section ended "on account of race, color, or previous condition of servitude." The wording was a compromise in both cases. It reinforced the nation's tradition that states set voter qualifications, but it imposed new federal rules about how that would be done. In 1920, states could no longer bar women from voting by writing "male" into a state's qualifications. That change, monumental as it was, left many women with US citizenship still unable to vote. To this day, they are vulnerable to state actions that exclude them for reasons other than race, color, or sex.

Early declarations of women's right to vote carried no instructions as to where women might secure it. Writing to a friend a few months after the meeting at Seneca Falls, Elizabeth Cady Stanton wondered: "We have declared our right to vote— The question now is how should we get possession of what rightfully belongs

"We have declared our right to vote— The question now is how should we get possession of what rightfully belongs to us?"

—Elizabeth Cady Stanton

to us?"[1] In the spring of 1850, women in Ohio offered one answer: they called a meeting in anticipation of a state constitutional convention and circulated petitions calling for the enfranchisement of women and Black men. Soon, pioneers in the women's rights movement were presenting their demand to state legislatures and conventions from New England to Kansas.[2]

States controlled access to the ballot box. Their constitutions defined who belonged to the club of voters and, by omission, who was excluded. They were not subtle. Wisconsin's first constitution in 1848 expressed ideas standard to the era:

Every male person of the age of twenty-one years or upwards, of the following classes, who shall have resided in this State for one year next preceding any election, shall be deemed a qualified elector at such election.

The eligible classes of adult males were "white citizens of the United States," white immigrants who had declared an intention to become citizens, and a small number of Native Americans not deemed to be tribal members. Neither females of those classes nor African Americans of either sex could qualify to vote. Across most of the country at midcentury the electorate was male, white, and over twenty-one.[3]

At the start of the Civil War in 1861, no women had gained voting rights. But this new movement had raised the topic of equal political rights in state and federal legal conversations. At war's end in 1865, that mattered. For women seeking equal rights, the postwar period of Reconstruction changed the political and legal landscape. The end of slavery required that citizenship be rethought. What is it and whose is it? Prior to ratification of the Fourteenth Amendment in 1868, the United States lacked a definition of who among its residents were citizens. The amendment's opening sentence addressed that gap:

All persons born or naturalized in the United States, and subject to the jurisdiction thereof, are citizens of the United States and of the State wherein they reside.

Though primarily aimed at recognizing African Americans as citizens, the language also removed any uncertainty about women's citizenship.[4] Questions remained, however, about what came with citizenship. Are voting rights inherent in citizenship? Is there a federal interest in voting rights? From 1865 to 1870, these questions were major topics of national debate.

At the start of the Civil War in 1861, no women had gained voting rights. But this new movement had raised the topic of equal political rights in state and federal legal conversations.

For most of that time, woman suffragists acted within an interracial equal rights movement. In many states of the North and the South, activists pressed to change state laws so that all adult men and women, Black and white, had equal rights to vote. Of hopes for New York in 1866, Susan B. Anthony told an audience: "now is the hour not only to demand suffrage for the negro, but for every other human being in the Republic."[5] Suffragists petitioned Congress to consider the advantages of universal suffrage tied to citizenship. In December 1868, Congressman George W. Julian of Indiana introduced language for an amendment that would achieve that ideal:

> *The right of suffrage in the United States shall be based on citizenship, and shall be regulated by Congress, and all citizens of the United States, whether native or naturalized, shall enjoy this right equally, without any distinction or discrimination whatever founded on race, color, or sex.*[6]

Julian envisaged not only a polity of equal rights among adult citizens, but also a federal government with the authority to qualify its voters.

This dream of voting rights for every citizen came to a splintered end. Congress rejected universal suffrage in favor of manhood suffrage. They proposed the Fifteenth Amendment as we know it to the states in February 1869, while women in the equal rights alliance were told to stand down. Allies who were willing to campaign for manhood suffrage took that path. African American women made choices between pressing for their individual rights or accepting that votes for freedmen alone was a huge leap forward. And woman suffrage lost its connection to a movement with universal aims. In short order, in March 1869, Congressman Julian introduced a sixteenth amendment for woman suffrage. Repeating his earlier language about suffrage and citizenship, he slimmed down the prohibitions to "founded on sex."[7] Congress let the matter drop.

Organizations devoted to winning woman suffrage date to this postwar period. Some of them were local groups, like the first one, in St. Louis. Within a few years, dozens of states boasted an association, sometimes two, if rivals for leadership could not get along. Two organizations with national ambitions were founded in 1869. One, calling itself the National Woman Suffrage Association, planned to keep pressure on the federal government to enfranchise women. This was the group led by Elizabeth Cady Stanton and Susan B. Anthony, among

Several lawyers argued that women had a right to vote because they were citizens. Activists, therefore, should challenge their exclusion from the ballot box through test cases in the courts.

many others. The
American Woman Suffrage
Association, led by Lucy Stone, accepted
the decision to leave women's rights to the
states. They resolved to work in that arena. If a major
state campaign were underway, as in Michigan in 1874,
both groups stepped up to help with speakers and funds.
These two associations survived for twenty-one years as
separate and often arguing entities.

Women in Vineland, New Jersey made their own ballot box from blueberry crates. They brought it to the polls beginning in November 1868, after they were prevented from voting the previous spring. Following that election, the president of the Historical Society of Vineland asked that the box be donated to the archives, along with the list of voters.

Formal organizations were not the sole drivers of
agitation about voting rights. Women took direct action
to claim their right to vote in a variety of ways, especially
in the hopeful years right after the war. In Vineland, New
Jersey, year after year, women installed their own ballot
box at the polling place and showed up on election day to
vote. In Lewiston, Maine, in fall 1868, a taxpaying widow
of a Union soldier applied to register as a voter. She was
one of many widows whose protests spotlighted their lack
of political representation. In Washington, DC, Frederick
Douglass marched with a large group of Black and white
women to the registrar of elections.[8]

The idea of a citizen's right to vote did not die with
Julian's amendment. Several lawyers argued that women
had a right to vote because they were citizens. Activists,
therefore, should challenge their exclusion from the
ballot box through test cases in the courts. In the early
1870s, what had been spontaneous actions by women to
show up at the polls became more systematic as women
planned lawsuits. At least six test cases reached the
courts—in California, Connecticut, Illinois, Missouri,
Pennsylvania, and the District of Columbia—and, after
state courts ruled against women, they appealed two

cases to the US Supreme Court.[9] Before the court heard arguments in the case of Virginia Minor of St. Louis, a different sort of case got underway in New York, after fourteen women in Rochester successfully registered and voted. The federal government arrested and indicted them. They were prosecuted for a criminal violation of federal law—voting without having the right to vote. Because one among them was very well known, the US attorney eventually proceeded only against her, and an associate justice of the Supreme Court presided at her trial.

Associate Justice Ward Hunt's opinion in that trial, *United States v. Susan B. Anthony* (1873), scoffed at the idea of a citizen's right to vote.

If the right belongs to any particular person, it is because such person is entitled to it by the laws of the State where he offers to exercise it, and not because of citizenship of the United States.

The states, he went on, could do what they wanted, provided their exclusions did not conflict with the Fifteenth Amendment.

If the State of New York should provide that no person should vote until he had reached the age of thirty years, . . . or that no person having gray hair, . . . should be entitled to vote, I do not see how it could be held to be a violation of any right derived or held under the Constitution of the United States.[10]

Susan B. Anthony was convicted of crime.

Eighteen months later, the Supreme Court heard the case of Virginia Minor. Denied registration as a voter, Minor wanted the court to rule that Missouri's limitation of voting rights to males was unconstitutional. In a unanimous opinion, the justices ruled that women were citizens of the country. They were thus "entitled to all the privileges and immunities of citizenship." That was a welcome clarification. But it begged the question, what are those privileges and immunities? In the court's view, they did not include voting rights. Writing in 1875, after ratification of the Fifteenth Amendment, the justices could agree

that the Constitution of the United States does not confer the right of suffrage upon any one, and that the constitutions and laws of the several States which commit that important trust to men alone are not necessarily void.[11]

Facing page: Virginia L. Minor and her husband, Francis Minor, of St. Louis sued for her right to vote in 1872 and appealed an adverse decision in Missouri to the Supreme Court of the United States. In 1875, the justices ruled that American citizenship did not confer voting rights on anyone and that states had a right to exclude women from voting.

The decisions in the cases of Susan B. Anthony and Virginia Minor not only closed a door for women but also opened doors for states. In advance of her trial, Susan B. Anthony had warned about the flawed reasoning:

> *It will not always be men combining to disfranchise all women. . . . Indeed, establish this precedent, admit this right to deny suffrage to the states, and there is no power to foresee the confusion, discord, and disruption that awaits us. There is, and can be, but one safe principle of government—equal rights to all.*[12]

Once the Supreme Court ruled against Virginia Minor, suffrage activism settled into two streams, federal and state. The National association returned to advocacy of a federal amendment. They used Julian's model with its claim of universal voting rights based on citizenship. However, in 1878, an amendment modeled on the Fifteenth Amendment was introduced in the Senate. Despite the less radical language, opponents blocked its consideration for nine years. On January 25, 1887, a day that coincided with a convention of woman suffragists in the nation's capital, Senator Henry W. Blair of New Hampshire brought the matter to the floor. The Senate finally voted on the issue. Women packed the Senate Gallery to watch senators defeat the resolution.[13] The Senate would not vote again on the amendment until 1914. In the House of Representatives, the amendment did not come up for any vote until 1915.

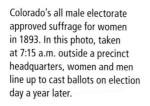

Colorado's all male electorate approved suffrage for women in 1893. In this photo, taken at 7:15 a.m. outside a precinct headquarters, women and men line up to cast ballots on election day a year later.

Meanwhile, the American association encouraged activists in states to pursue any political rights that fell within a state's power to grant. Suffragists poured enormous resources into state and territorial campaigns, with far more lost than won. But the wins mattered to the women in the West who gained a voice in government through full suffrage.

Woman suffragists did not act in a political vacuum but were influenced and constrained by national politics. In the South, the withdrawal of federal troops as part of the Compromise of 1877 closed Reconstruction and reversed the progress toward political participation made by African Americans in that region. Elections in southern states were occasions of racial violence. Federal enforcement of the Fifteenth Amendment ceased, and white southerners regained power in Congress. States in the former Confederacy set about rewriting their constitutions to put obstacles in the way of African American men registering to vote. Beginning with Mississippi's new constitution of 1890, the states defined an assortment of ways to block or significantly reduce Black enfranchisement.

At about the same time, after the Senate vote on a woman suffrage amendment in 1887, discussion began about merging the two suffrage associations before their leaders died. There were lots of reasons. But the defeat of the amendment seemed to signal the end of an old divide and a chance for suffragists to unite around state action. Through merger, the National American Woman Suffrage Association came into existence in 1890. Attention to federal protection for a citizen's right to vote or any federal amendment waned.

It happened, then, that in 1890, woman suffragists stopped seeking federal protection for voting rights at the same moment that southern states formalized the exclusion of Black men from the franchise. Their complicity went further. To gain ground in the white South, the National American Woman Suffrage Association affirmed in 1903 its belief in the South's prerogative to legislate white supremacy. The association resolved, it seeks "to do away with the requirement of a sex qualification for suffrage. . . . What other qualifications shall be asked for it leaves to each State."[14] The political equality of all citizens was no longer the organized movement's objective.

Woman suffragists turned back to the goal of a constitutional amendment in 1913 and the Senate voted on the measure in 1914—defeating it again. But this time, despite a persistent interest in keeping the focus on state actions and despite a new divide between two

Woman suffragists did not act in a political vacuum but were influenced and constrained by national politics.

suffrage groups, women stayed the course. They kept up pressure until both houses of Congress approved the measure in June 1919. It is this last phase, from 1913 to 1919, that produces the most striking stories and martyrology of woman suffrage history, with jail sentences, hunger strikes, and forced feeding. The images shocked contemporaries and clothed the federal government as oppressor. Less colorful was the fact that by 1919 women in fifteen states had gained full voting rights and were electing senators and members of Congress. The men who were accountable to female constituents voted overwhelmingly in support of the amendment. Like any amendment proposed to the Constitution, this one needed three-quarters of the states (thirty-six at the time) to ratify it. Those many steps took more than a year and came down to one vote in one state—in Tennessee in August 1920. It had taken decades and generations to eliminate the *presumption* that men had a right to govern for women. Activists had changed both law and political culture because they believed that manhood suffrage—full voting rights for men and only men—made a mockery of self-government.

This huge step toward "a more perfect union" left standing the judicial decisions that a right to vote was *not* a fundamental right of American citizenship. Although the National Woman's Party had referred to the Nineteenth Amendment as the "Susan B. Anthony Amendment," it did not reflect her convictions about a citizen's right to vote. The difference was underscored immediately in the fall of 1920 by the federal government's decision that the women of Puerto Rico, despite their US citizenship, were not enfranchised by the amendment because citizenship did not guarantee a right to vote.[15] Their woman suffrage movement lasted until 1935.

The amendment also left in place states' rights to exclude citizens from the rolls of eligible voters provided that the reasons for doing so were not those itemized in the Fifteenth and Nineteenth Amendments. This bow to states' rights was a part of the amendment's political appeal and is a part of its legacy to this day. This amendment

US Secretary of State Bainbridge Colby signed the Nineteenth Amendment into law from his home in Washington, DC on August 26, 1920. It was announced in that city's Evening Star that same day. The reference to a "50 Year Struggle" counts back to the ratification of the Fifteenth Amendment and early hopes of similar federal action for women.

SUFFRAGE PROCLAIMED BY COLBY, WHO SIGNS AT HOME EARLY IN DAY

'50 - Year Struggle Ends in Victory for Women

NO CEREMONY IN FINAL ACTION

Secretary Felicitates Leaders; Hails New Era.

simply meant that the state must discriminate equally. As the Equal Suffrage League of Virginia reassured the white public in 1916, speaking of the devices by which African Americans were kept at bay, "as these qualifications restrict the negro man's vote, it stands to reason that they will also restrict the negro woman's vote."[16]

In northern states, African American women embraced their new right to vote and used its power to press for racial justice and equality. The experience of African American women in states of the former Confederacy was not uniform. It took several years for officials to complete the job of disfranchisement. Some women managed to register and vote in the presidential election in 1920. But across much of the South, equal discrimination subjected African American women to well-practiced tactics designed to discourage and/or disqualify them as voters. William Pickens, of the National Association for the Advancement of Colored People, reported on voter registration in Columbia, South Carolina, a state where African Americans made up the majority of the population. Registrars were surprised at the high numbers of Black women who lined up to register, he wrote.

They relied on a familiar tactic, "white people first," leaving women of color standing for hours. On the second day, these women "were made to read and even to explain long passages from the constitutions and from various civil and criminal codes."[17] White supremacists of South Carolina followed the path etched in Ward Hunt's conviction of Susan B. Anthony, the same one later ratified by the National American Woman Suffrage Association's promise to the South in 1903, that states could invent whatever qualifications for voters they desired, so long as there was no sex qualification. It took forty-five years to win the Voting Rights Act of 1965 that protected the rights for people of color, women and men, across the South.

To close the history of woman suffrage at 1920 is to ignore those women left behind in 1920, women who still dreamed of equal political rights. It is also to ignore how precarious the victory, how easily women can lose their ability to vote if the state where they reside exercises its right to exclude people, and to forget that freedom without voting rights is a mockery, whoever you are.

Like any amendment proposed to the Constitution, this one needed three-quarters of the states (thirty-six at the time) to ratify it. Those many steps took more than a year and came down to one vote in one state—in Tennessee in August 1920. It had taken decades and generations to eliminate the presumption that men had a right to govern for women.

Jessie Jack Hooper

Jessie Jack Hooper was an influential suffragist living in Oshkosh, Wisconsin. She was president of the Wisconsin Woman Suffrage Association and was also a member of the National American Woman Suffrage Association (NAWSA). Hooper worked with movement leaders such as Carrie Chapman Catt and Dr. Anna Howard Shaw. Her presence in the movement and in the political arena paved the way for future women voters and politicians.

Born in Iowa in 1865, Jessie Jack moved to Wisconsin after marrying Ben Hooper. She grew frustrated with life in Oshkosh as city officials often ignored the needs of women residents. Without the vote, women had little power in civic life. Hooper realized that elected leaders would only take women seriously if they had suffrage (voting) rights.

After this realization, Jessie Jack Hooper devoted her full attention to the women's suffrage movement. She spent much of her time traveling throughout the state, promoting suffrage rights. She was also a frequent speaker at the Capitol Building in Madison. Hooper served as a board member of NAWSA and spent much of her time in Washington, DC.

Along with other suffragists, Hooper visited members of Congress to convince them to support women's suffrage. She is largely responsible for influencing state legislators to vote on the Nineteenth Amendment, which recognized women's suffrage rights. As a result of her efforts, Wisconsin became the first state to ratify the amendment.

After the amendment was ratified in August of 1920, Hooper spent her energy on promoting world peace. She ran for a seat in the US Senate in 1922. Hooper lost the race to Robert La Follette, yet her foray into politics paved the wave for many future female politicians. Due to her prominence in the women's suffrage movement, Hooper's house in Oshkosh is listed on the National Register of Historic Places.

Associated Places:
Jessie Jack Hooper House, Oshkosh, Wisconsin (on the National Register of Historic Places)

Wisconsin State Capitol, Madison, Wisconsin (on the National Register of Historic Places and designated a National Historic Landmark)

—Katherine Crawford-Lackey

The Necessity of Other Social Movements to the Struggle for Woman Suffrage

by Robyn Muncy

A merican women's struggle for the vote was a profoundly important chapter in the story of American democracy. But it did not unfold as an independent plot. Instead, the woman suffrage movement emerged from and was continually fed by other social movements and political causes.[1] Between the 1830s and 1920, women's enfranchisement was intimately connected to such crusades as the struggle for racial justice, the women's rights movement, the campaign to regulate alcohol, and the labor movement.[2] For some women, involvement in these social movements created the very desire for the vote. For many, it honed skills necessary to building a political movement. At various points, factions within those social movements became allies of the suffrage campaign, expanding its base of support. Many of these movements circulated ideas about human rights and democracy that prompted increasing numbers of Americans to advocate women's enfranchisement. In all these ways, other reform movements were crucial to the victories of woman suffrage.

In all these ways, other reform movements were crucial to the victories of woman suffrage.

* * *

The antebellum period (the years before the Civil War), was awash in religious fervor, economic upheaval, and debates over the meaning of the American Revolution. It generated many potent reform movements. Women's participation in these movements often nudged them beyond the domestic sphere, accepted in the early nineteenth century as women's natural place. Sometimes this activism eroded their acceptance of social norms that required women's subordination to men. In fact, during the 1840s and 1850s, a women's rights movement coalesced from a wide array of other antebellum reform drives. This women's rights movement eventually produced a sustained struggle for woman suffrage.

The antislavery movement, the most significant antebellum reform effort, proved a powerful generator of women's rights activism. A fundamental institution of American life at the birth of the republic, slavery

Copper antislavery token dated 1838, struck by Gibbs, Gardner, and Company for the American Anti-Slavery Society. It reads, "Am I Not A Woman & A Sister." Such tokens were sold at fundraising events organized by female antislavery activists.

became ever more central to the US economy during the early nineteenth century. Organized opposition to slavery emerged first among free Blacks in the North, as well as Quakers, Unitarians, and evangelical Christians, both Black and white. Radical abolitionism publicly debuted in 1829 when African American David Walker published *Walker's Appeal, In Four Articles*. This work was a forceful critique of slavery and racial discrimination. Two years later, white New Englander William Lloyd Garrison began publishing the *Liberator*. In 1833, he joined with other opponents of slavery to form the American Anti-Slavery Society (AASS). The AASS demanded the immediate abolition of slavery and full civil rights for African Americans. Its broad commitment to human rights opened the AASS to overtures by women for voice and leadership. Over one hundred local women's affiliates joined the cause.[3]

The *Liberator* demonstrated its openness to women in 1831 when it published an essay by Maria Stewart, a free Black woman. Stewart condemned slavery as well as discrimination against free Blacks and women. She urged free Black men, "sue for your rights and privileges." And she asked, "How long shall the fair daughters of Africa be compelled to bury their minds and talents beneath a load of iron pots and kettles?"[4] When a Boston antislavery society invited Stewart to speak in 1832, she became the first American-born woman to address an audience of both women and men. By doing so, Stewart violated social conventions that forbade women from speaking before what was termed a "promiscuous" audience. Women might speak before a gathering of women in their parlors or churches, but an audience of both women and men outraged propriety. Stewart left Boston in 1833, disappointed that the city seemed to reject her leadership. But the publication of her works by the *Liberator* assured that her anti-racist, abolitionist feminism reached beyond Boston. Her public addresses set a precedent for other female activists.[5]

Stewart's ideas certainly resonated with those of the interracial Philadelphia Female Anti-Slavery Society. It was founded the very year that Stewart left Boston. Philadelphia was a hotbed of antislavery activism in part because of its vital Quaker community, which was inclined to egalitarian social relations by the belief that God dwelled in every person.[6] Quaker egalitarianism even helped to convert two women born to the southern plantation elite, Angelina and Sarah Grimké, to antislavery activism. In 1836, after living in Philadelphia for several years, the sisters took up the abolitionist cause. They soon scandalized many Americans by speaking before gender- and race-integrated audiences, as Maria Stewart had. Their audacity provoked violent opposition.[7]

The belief of many women in the antislavery movement that God called them to the cause weakened their acceptance of cultural prohibitions against women's public activism.[8] Some antislavery activists even began to see the exclusion of women from public life as a violation of women's own human rights. By 1838, Sarah Grimké came to the conclusion that "Men and women were CREATED EQUAL; they are both moral and accountable beings; and whatever is *right* for man to do, is *right* for woman."[9] Some of those who could not countenance this perfect equality of women and men nevertheless questioned limitations on women's freedom to work publicly to benefit others. After all, dominant ideals of womanhood assumed women's selflessness and innate moral perspicacity. If God granted women special moral insight, some asked, did it make sense to ban women from public life, which so desperately needed moral leadership?

So contentious did women's roles become among abolitionists that they split over the issue in 1840. Those accepting women's rights as a legitimate commitment for their movement remained in the AASS. Those opposed formed the American and Foreign Anti-Slavery Society. From that point on, women

Charlotte Forten Grimké, member of a prominent African American family in Philadelphia. The women of the Forten family, including Charlotte's mother, grandmother, and three aunts, were central to founding the Philadelphia Female Anti-Slavery Society.

such as Lucretia Mott and Lydia Maria Child were elected officers of the AASS. Others, including Susan B. Anthony, were hired as paid organizers.[10] In this way, the antislavery movement became a significant node in the emerging network of activists demanding greater power and scope for American women.

There were many other nodes. One was the labor movement. Textile manufacturing industrialized in the early nineteenth century. Factories recruited young women from rural families to work in the new cloth-making mills that dotted New England. In the 1830s, those earliest of America's industrial workers staged strikes against deteriorating working conditions, claiming a public voice and presence for working women.[11] In that same decade, both Black and white women, working and middle class, joined a movement for moral reform. These activists decried social norms that allowed respectable men to frequent brothels while condemning prostitutes as hopeless sinners. Moral reformers wanted men held to the same chaste standard as women and to offer alternative employment opportunities to poor women. This move-ment critiqued the existing gender system and slid some women reformers into public life.[12] Like moral reform, the temperance movement urged men to control their desire for pleasure, in this case by abstaining from drunkenness. Some women saw temperance as an issue on which they must take a public stand in order to protect their families from domestic violence and poverty. The antebellum temperance movement became another site for reimagin-ing women's proper place in society. It gave some women experience in public speaking and movement organizing.[13]

The antebellum period also witnessed indepen-dent campaigns explicitly for women's rights. Frances Wright began lecturing about the equality of women and men soon after her immigration to the United States from Scotland in the 1820s. Her efforts produced no sustained following, probably because she rejected marriage and supported racial equality.[14] But other, more focused drives won adherents. Calls for equal access to education and employment, for instance, drew broader support.[15] Demands for equal pay resonated power-fully among women teachers.[16] Agitation for married women's property rights gained momentum when, in 1836, Ernestine Rose, a Jewish immigrant from Poland by way of England, campaigned in New York for a law aimed at securing married women's property rights. The proposal represented change because, when women in the United States married, they generally lost con-trol of their property and even the wages they earned.

The antebellum temperance movement became another site for reimagining women's proper place in society. It gave some women experience in public speaking and movement organizing.

Husbands controlled all under the legal doctrine of coverture. This doctrine said that women had no independent legal identity once married. In the 1840s, emerging feminists Paulina Wright and Elizabeth Cady Stanton joined Rose in lobbying for married women's economic rights in New York. They achieved partial success in 1848 and a broader triumph in 1860.[7]

At the same time, Stanton, a privileged and brilliant mother deeply dissatisfied with the restrictions on antebellum women's lives, imagined a broader agenda. Strong ties to antislavery Quakers made it possible for Stanton to organize support for her vision of greater equality for women. Her activist friends included Lucretia Mott, whom Stanton had first met in 1840 at the World Anti-Slavery Convention in London, Martha Coffin Wright, Mott's sister, Mary Ann and Elizabeth M'Clintock, and Jane Hunt. Together, these women called the first women's rights convention in US history. It convened at Seneca Falls, New York, in July 1848. Over three hundred participants, men and women, Black and white, attended that historic two-day meeting. They debated the Declaration of Sentiments, a sweeping list of demands for women's advancement. These demands ranged from equal access to education and professions to married women's property rights and access to divorce—as well as the vote. All the demands passed unanimously except the call for suffrage. Only passionate advocacy by Stanton and antislavery activist Frederick Douglass saved that item from the scrap heap. Clearly, suffrage was not, in the 1840s, a central issue even for many women's rights advocates. Nevertheless, the vote commonly appeared on the agendas of national women's rights conventions that began in 1850.[18]

Suffrage became a central concern of the women's rights movement because of the allied movement for racial justice. The US Civil War interrupted the campaign for women's rights between 1861 and 1865. But once slavery was legally abolished and the US Congress began to debate the civil and political rights of freed people, women's rights agitation reemerged. During a congressional push for the protection of Black men's voting rights, some advocates of African American and women's rights formed the American Equal Rights Association. This group pressed for the simultaneous enfranchisement of Black men and all women. (By that point, the states had generally enfranchised all white men.) When it became clear, however, that Congress would, through the Fifteenth Amendment, protect the voting rights of Black men but not those of women,

Suffrage became a central concern of the women's rights movement because of the allied movement for racial justice.

Presentation Committee of the Woman's Christian Temperance Union of Illinois, ca. 1879. Frances Willard, president of the WCTU from 1879 to 1898, is in the center of this photograph, which also features one of the organization's home protection petitions.

some women's rights activists, including Elizabeth Cady Stanton and Susan B. Anthony, refused to support it. They formed the National Woman Suffrage Association to push for a Sixteenth Amendment enfranchising women. Activists committed to maintaining the alliance between the movements for racial justice and women's rights, especially Lucy Stone and Julia Ward Howe, formed the American Woman Suffrage Association. It supported the Fifteenth Amendment and mounted state-level battles for women's enfranchisement. Not until 1890 would the two groups reunite in the National American Woman Suffrage Association, which became the principal woman suffrage organization in the decades leading to ratification of Nineteenth Amendment.[19] By that time, the alliance between the movements for racial justice and women's rights was severely attenuated.

As women's rights advocates split over their relationship to racial justice, the woman suffrage effort received a boost from another social movement, the temperance crusade. Founded in the 1870s, the Woman's Christian Temperance Union (WCTU) became the largest women's organization in the late nineteenth century. Especially strong in the Midwest and South, the WCTU focused on closing saloons through nonviolent direct action and laws limiting the sale of alcohol. In 1876, one of the WCTU's leaders, Frances Willard, concluded that women would have greater power to win temperance legislation if they had the vote. She did not claim the franchise as a right, however, but as a necessity for fulfilling women's domestic duties. While in prayer, Willard wrote in her autobiography, she received the revelation that she should "speak for the woman's ballot as a weapon of protection to her home."[20] With that framing, in 1881 Willard convinced the WCTU to endorse woman suffrage. As a result, many socially conservative women began to support their own voting rights, expanding the movement's base.[21] Indeed, because so many women backed temperance, the Prohibition Party endorsed woman suffrage in 1872. It remained a staunch supporter of the movement for decades.

The Populist Party was another third-party advocate of votes for women. A coalition of farmers, workers, and small business owners opposed to the control of the US economy by an eastern corporate elite, the Populist Party in 1892 proposed a set of policies intended to broaden American democracy and democratize the US economy. The enfranchisement of women was on that agenda. The victory of woman suffrage in Colorado in 1893 can be directly credited to the Populists. Several men in Colorado, including juvenile court judge Benjamin Lindsey, became national spokesmen for women's enfranchisement.[22]

Although the Populist Party disappeared into the Democratic Party in 1896, many of its commitments were absorbed by the Progressive movement that emerged in the 1890s. This movement dominated American politics in the early twentieth century. The Progressive movement began in diffuse local initiatives aimed to diminish the egregious inequalities of wealth and power created by new national corporations. By the 1890s, these economic behemoths controlled entire sectors of the US economy and wielded substantial political power. Women were prominent among local reformers who tried to rein in corporate power through state laws to limit working hours, regulate child labor, and institute factory safety measures. Those same reformers also expanded public education, built public playgrounds, and created a juvenile justice system. They eventually created a federal income tax and public programs to reduce maternal and infant mortality. By the 1910s, many women in the Progressive movement were national political leaders. These included Mary Church Terrell, first president of the National Association of Colored

Women were prominent among local reformers who tried to rein in corporate power through state laws to limit working hours, regulate child labor, and institute factory safety measures.

Women; Jane Addams, champion of working-class families; Florence Kelley, head of the National Consumers League; and Ida B. Wells-Barnett, anti-lynching crusader and cofounder of the National Association for the Advancement of Colored People (NAACP).[23]

As millions of American women worked passionately in the Progressive movement, many came to believe, as had so many female abolitionists and temperance advocates, that they needed the vote in order to succeed in their other reform efforts. Some also believed that women deserved the vote as a matter of right. Either way, these reformers swelled the ranks of the woman suffrage movement. Their visibility and effectiveness as reformers also meant that Progressive men increasingly supported votes for women. In fact, the Progressive Party of 1912, an enormously important third-party effort, endorsed woman suffrage, Its presidential nominee, former president Theodore Roosevelt, proclaimed that women would participate in the Progressive Party on a basis of "absolute equality" with men.[24]

Although African American suffragists worked vigorously for the cause in the early twentieth century, the deterioration of US race relations after 1890—embodied in brutal measures to segregate the races and disfranchise African American men in the South—meant that suffragists worked mostly in racially segregated organizations between 1890 and 1920. While white suffragists, including some who expressly opposed the enfranchisement of Black women, increased the membership of NAWSA to two million, many Black women worked for the vote through multifocus organizations such as the National Association of Colored Women or the Women's Convention of the Black Baptist Church. Ida B. Wells-Barnett founded the Alpha Suffrage Club in Chicago. It contributed mightily to the victory of woman suffrage in Illinois (1913). The NAACP, organized in 1909–10, became an important forum for suffrage activism that included both woman suffrage and the reenfranchisement of Black men in the South.[25]

Women in the labor movement and Socialist Party also expanded support for woman suffrage in the early twentieth century. Immigrant women in New York's garment industry, including Clara Lemlich, Rose Schneiderman, and Pauline Newman, agitated for the vote. Although many male labor leaders and Socialists supported woman suffrage in principle, they did not make it a priority. Indeed, many belittled woman suffrage as a middle-class issue. But leaders among the dramatically increasing group of working women

Facing page: Rose Schneiderman, who emigrated from eastern Europe as a child, became an important labor leader in New York and a much-sought-after suffrage speaker. She helped to win full suffrage for women in New York in 1917.

Relationships between the woman suffrage movement and other social movements were sometimes wrenching. Witness the conflict over the Fifteenth Amendment and the racial and class segregation of most suffrage organizations in the early twentieth century. Even so, the suffrage movement owed its existence and much of its gradually increasing strength to other reform movements.

argued that wage-earning women needed the vote. Only with suffrage, they insisted, could working women hope for equal pay, safe work places, and humane hours. In 1909, working-class suffragists generated a major debate about their cause within New York's labor community. In 1911 they formed the Wage Earners' League for Woman Suffrage.[26] One of the league's flyers asked, "Why are you paid less than a man? Why do you work in a fire trap? Why are your hours so long?" The answer: "Because you are a woman and have no vote. Votes make the law. The law controls conditions. Women who want better conditions must vote."[27] Woman suffrage triumphed in New York in 1917 partly because so many working-class men voted yes.[28] Similar agitation occurred elsewhere to such an extent that throughout the 1910s, working-class men memorialized Congress to pass a woman suffrage amendment to the Constitution.[29] Likewise in the territories. Puerto Rican labor activist Luisa Capetillo argued so effectively for woman suffrage that by 1908 the island's Free Federation of Workers endorsed women's enfranchisement, and wage-earning women and the Socialist Party were among the most ardent suffrage activists.[30]

* * *

Relationships between the woman suffrage movement and other social movements were sometimes wrenching. Witness the conflict over the Fifteenth Amendment and the racial and class segregation of most suffrage organizations in the early twentieth century. Even so, the suffrage movement owed its existence and much of its gradually increasing strength to other reform movements. A host of antebellum reform efforts drew female adherents out of the domestic sphere, challenging prevailing gender conventions and motivating many to ask questions about all the restrictions on their lives. The accumulation of those questions—and experience with writing, speaking, and organizing—produced a women's movement that eventually put suffrage front and center. Moreover, the fervent desire to change American life— whether by increasing women's wages or decreasing alcohol consumption—encouraged many women between the 1830s and 1920 to desire the vote as an important tool in their quest to perfect the union. Male colleagues in those reform movements increasingly perceived the value to their own political causes of enfranchising the women who worked alongside them. In sum, other reform movements were crucial to the victory of votes for women.

The Justice Bell

The Justice Bell, a (near) replica of the Liberty Bell, was used to promote women's suffrage across the United States. The bell is also known as the Women's Liberty Bell and the Suffrage Bell. Katherine Wentworth Ruschenberger commissioned the bell in 1915. She was one of the 70,000 members of the Pennsylvania Woman Suffrage Association, and a leader of the organization in Chester County.

A close replica of the Liberty Bell (on display at Independence National Historical Park), the bronze Justice Bell was cast without a crack. The inscription on the Justice Bell reads:

> **ESTABLISH JUSTICE**
> **PROCLAIM LIBERTY**
> **THROUGHOUT ALL THE LAND UNTO ALL THE**
> **INHABITANTS THEREOF**
> **MENEELY BELL CO**
> **TROY, NY**
> **MCMXV**

The bell was cast by the Meneely Bell Foundry in Troy, New York.

After production, the bell was mounted on the bed of a pick-up truck and taken on a driving tour to all of Pennsylvania's 67 counties. Its clapper (the part that hits the bell to make a sound) was chained, preventing the bell from ringing. This symbolized the silence of women who did not have the vote. The bell's 5,000 mile road trip was designed to raise awareness for women's suffrage in Pennsylvania – a state-wide referendum that failed in 1915.[1,2]

In 1920, women took the bell on the road again, traveling to several states to raise support for the ratification of the Nineteenth Amendment. After the Nineteenth Amendment was ratified in August 1920, a celebration was held on the steps of Independence Hall in Philadelphia. The Justice Bell was rung 48 times – once for every state in the union (Alaska and Hawai'i became states after 1920).

The Justice Bell is on permanent display at Washington Memorial Chapel, Valley Forge, Pennsylvania. Although located within the boundaries of Valley Forge National Historical Park, the Washington Memorial Chapel is technically not part of the park itself.[3]

Associated Places:
Independence National Historical Park, Philadelphia, Pennsylvania

Valley Forge National Historical Park, Pennsylvania

—Katherine Crawford-Lackey

Flexing Feminine Muscles: Strategies and Conflicts in the Suffrage Movement

by Susan Goodier

Winning women's right to vote took the energies of three generations of women, the support of a few men, and nearly a century to accomplish. The process necessitated that suffragists ally with groups holding other priorities. These included abolitionists, temperance and maternalist reformers, and eventually political and third-party reformers. The result was broader support. When they began in the early nineteenth century, suffragists argued from a natural rights perspective. After the Civil War, during Reconstruction, suffragists cited the importance of women's unique characteristics as justification for the vote while also demanding the vote for themselves as citizens. Then, as suffragists observed the success of women's enfranchisement in the West, they increasingly focused on justice and equality arguments.

Meanwhile southerners' tightening of Jim Crow legal restrictions, which constrained African American voting and other rights, led some suffragists to develop arguments that played upon racial fears. Over the course of the movement, suffragists continually modified their strategies. They relied on state and national conventions, parlor meetings, petitions, promotional stunts, and print culture. Conflict, inherent to all social justice movements, stimulated ever greater creativity and influenced the strategies women drew upon. By the first two decades of the twentieth century, suffragists had become experts at marketing their movement. They overcame most conflicts with careful strategizing.

A century earlier, during an era of "parlor politics," women sought to influence powerful men in private settings. A few daring women, such as Fanny Wright, spoke on lecture circuits and published their ideas. In these early years of the movement, suffragists looked back to the American Revolution to ground their idea that women were citizens and had the same natural rights as men. Because the government derived from the "consent of the governed," as stated in the Declaration of Independence, women must be included in the electorate. The cry "no taxation without representation" applied to women as well as men. Democratic ideals of equality between races, as well as the growing abolition movement, also

Winning women's right to vote took the energies of three generations of women, the support of a few men, and nearly a century to accomplish.

influenced ideas related to gender equality. Wright, a
freethinker, demanded that women be given an education
equal to that of men. African American abolitionist Maria W.
Stewart argued for the need to educate young women of
color. Abolitionists and women's rights activists Sarah and
Angelina Grimké, who spoke to mixed audiences (made
up of women and men), and Margaret Fuller, author
of *Woman in the Nineteenth Century* (1845), called for
equality between women and men. By 1846, six property-
owning women submitted a petition to the New York
State Constitutional Convention. It demanded that the
Convention confer upon women the same "equal, and civil
and political rights" white men enjoyed.[1] Two years later,
in July 1848, five women, including Quakers Lucretia Mott,
her sister Martha Coffin Wright, Jane Hunt, and Mary
M'Clintock, along with Elizabeth Cady Stanton, organized
a women's rights convention in Seneca Falls, New York.
Three hundred women and men responded to the call.
They traveled from across the state to discuss the "social,
civil and religious condition and rights of woman."[2] The
organizers drafted a Declaration of Sentiments based on
the wording of the Declaration of Independence. It called
for greater civic and political rights for women.

During two days of debate, attendees supported
most of the Declaration's resolutions. Mott had forewarned
Stanton that a demand for women's enfranchisement
would likely put other goals of the convention at risk. As
predicted, activists argued strenuously over inclusion of a
demand for woman suffrage. Frederick Douglass and a few
others finally convinced those in attendance to support
the resolution—although they expected "misconception,

*The Age of Brass/Or the Triumph's
of Woman's Rights.* This Currier
and Ives lithograph highlights
the fears many people had about
women's rights.

misrepresentation, and ridicule." They determined to circulate tracts, petition legislators, curry the support of religious leaders and the press, and travel the speaking circuits. Immediately planning for additional conventions, activists eventually expected to hold them nationwide.[3] For a dozen years, women's rights conventions drew the curious and the interested.

Efforts to gain women's rights, however, stalled during the Civil War. Rather than continue to petition and hold conventions for woman suffrage, many women chose to prove they were essential to the war effort. By extension, they also saw themselves as essential to the political process.[4] Stanton and Susan B. Anthony founded the Women's Loyal National League in 1863 to support the war and the end of slavery. Women served as nurses in field hospitals, while others ran farms or businesses left behind when men enlisted or were drafted. Energetic women organized fairs under the auspices of the United States Sanitary Commission to raise money to support the Union.[5] Although they wholeheartedly supported the Union cause, women's rights activists expected to be rewarded for their efforts with full citizenship rights. They believed these rights should include the right to vote.

At war's end, the link between women's rights and rights for freed people remained. This shaped postwar strategies and conflicts. At the 1866 national women's rights convention, the first since before the war, white and Black reformers founded the American Equal Rights Association (AERA). The purpose was to secure suffrage "irrespective of race, color, or sex." Lucretia Mott, known for

Facing page: Mrs. W. J. Roach, Mrs. E. J. Graham, and Mrs. W. I. Scott sell copies of the *Woman's Journal* in New Orleans, ca. 1910s.

Suffrage leaders formulated a legal strategy they called the "new departure." They argued that suffrage was one of the "privileges or immunities" of citizenship protected by the Fourteenth Amendment.

her commitment to equal rights and her ability to mediate between opposing factions, served as president.[6] Association members traveled the lecture circuit, even influencing some southern states to consider equal rights.[7] With the Fourteenth Amendment, legislators tied representation in Congress to the number of male voters. As a result, suffragists divided over their loyalties.[8] The 1869 AERA convention took place during congressional debates on the Fifteenth Amendment to enfranchise Black men. At the convention, Douglass, Stanton, Anthony, and Massachusetts suffrage leaders Lucy Stone and Henry Blackwell argued vehemently. Stone reasoned that enfranchisement for Black men signified progress, while Stanton and Anthony contended that woman suffrage was equally important and should not be sacrificed. The AERA underwent a painful split.[9]

Two new organizations resulted. They grew in strength and political expertise as their leadership developed increasingly effective ways to promote woman suffrage. Anthony and Stanton immediately established the National Woman Suffrage Association (NWSA) with an all-female membership. They demanded a sixteenth amendment enfranchising citizens without regard to sex. Their weekly newspaper, the *Revolution*, publicized their views on woman suffrage, politics, labor, and other subjects.[10] By September, rivals Stone and Blackwell founded the less militant American Woman Suffrage Association (AWSA).[11] Its members, which included women and men, focused on state campaigns to demand or expand woman suffrage, staying away from other issues. Stone also began the *Woman's Journal* in 1870, which became the most successful and longest lasting suffrage newspaper. Whether states or the federal government should dictate who had the right to vote remained a contentious issue throughout the movement.

Black women activists divided their allegiance between the AWSA and the NWSA. Sojourner Truth and Harriet Tubman attended NWSA conventions, while Charlotte Forten and Frances Ellen Watkins Harper supported the AWSA.[12] Although most Black women's benevolent and literary clubs supported suffrage for women, Sarah Smith Thompson Garnet founded the first known organization of Black women devoted specifically to suffrage. Called the Brooklyn Colored Woman's Equal Suffrage League, she founded it in the late 1880s.[13] African American suffragists operated in dynamic networks of support in Black communities in cities throughout the nation but tended to work outside the mainstream movement. This was in part because white women, particularly in the South, rarely welcomed their Black sisters.[14]

Suffragists employed ever more complex strategies to promote women's enfranchisement. Suffrage leaders formulated a legal strategy they called the "new departure." They argued that suffrage was one of the "privileges or immunities" of citizenship protected by the Fourteenth Amendment. From 1868 to 1872, hundreds of Black and white women suffragists registered and voted, hoping to bring the issue before the courts. Officials arrested many of these women, who then filed suit—or were charged with a crime. Sojourner Truth, Sarah Grimké, her niece Angelina Grimké Weld, Matilda Joslyn Gage, and many other less well-known women engaged in this strategy. The most famous of these was Susan B. Anthony, who, along with fourteen other women, voted in an 1872 election in Rochester, New York.[15] Her trial resulted in a guilty verdict and a fine she refused to pay.[16] Virginia Minor of Missouri further tested the understanding of citizenship as plaintiff in *Minor v. Happersett* in the 1874 United States Supreme Court. Justices unanimously determined that the Fourteenth Amendment did not intend that woman suffrage be guaranteed. The case marked a serious setback not just for the woman suffrage movement, but for civil rights of all citizens. The result was refocused attention on a federal amendment.[17]

After years of hard work, in 1887 members of the NWSA and legislative supporters finally brought a proposal for a federal amendment to a vote in Congress. It failed. This prompted suffragists to revise their strategies yet again, beginning with uniting disparate suffrage factions. Lucy Stone and her daughter, Alice Stone Blackwell, began negotiations with Susan B. Anthony to merge the AWSA and the NWSA.[18] The process took more than two years. Many leaders, such as Matilda Joslyn Gage of New York and Olympia Brown of Wisconsin, who feared the loss of attention to a federal amendment, opposed the merger.[19] Nevertheless, the two groups became the National American Woman Suffrage Association (NAWSA) in February 1890.[20] Many state and local political equality and suffrage clubs, once affiliated with one or the other of the former associations, formalized their affiliation with the new association.[21]

NAWSA had a total of four presidents: Elizabeth Cady Stanton, Susan B. Anthony, Carrie Chapman Catt in two separate terms, and Anna Howard Shaw. Each had her own strategy. Stanton, chosen primarily to honor her, spent most of her term in England with her

Strategies women in the West utilized mirrored those used in the East. These included lobbying, participating in parades and meetings, supporting the party that endorsed woman suffrage, forming coalitions, and increasing the respectability of women's voting.

Women opposed to woman suffrage published articles in lady's magazines; others frustrated suffragists by their indifference.

daughter. Anthony, who had already taken on presidential duties, hoped the organization would prioritize a federal amendment, although state and local suffrage activity often siphoned energy and attention from a national focus.[22] She also had the support of Frances Willard's Woman's Christian Temperance Union. The largest women's organization in the world, the union endorsed woman suffrage on the premise that having the vote would help protect women and children from problems related to alcohol.[23] Catt, who served from 1900 until 1904, then again beginning in 1908, focused on attracting elite women's money and support. She also worked to educate confident suffrage speakers and organizers tasked with establishing suffrage clubs. Shaw, who spoke before an estimated million people during her tenure, challenged the "Southern strategy" of the 1890s. This strategy explicitly connected woman suffrage to white supremacy to court southern support. Shaw understood the hypocrisy of a strategy that would exclude any race or class from the right to vote.[24]

The country became ever more industrialized and urbanized in the late nineteenth century. As immigration brought increasing diversity, class and ethnic divisions undermined an assumed male equality. White supremacist rule returned to the southern states, increasing racially-based violence. Simultaneously, suffragists argued that the nation would benefit from women's selflessness, devotion to family, and social benevolence. Some women, especially those who also supported temperance, claimed they needed the ballot for self-protection or to meet social reform goals. Many elite, white suffragists advocated for restricted suffrage. They promoted the idea of enfranchising educated white women but not the "undesirable" classes (immigrants and Blacks) as a solution.[25] So, while many women had come to support suffrage, they sometimes did so from dramatically different perspectives.

As the United States expanded westward, new territories and states entered the union. Women were often already entitled to the vote in these new states. Strategies women in the West utilized mirrored those used in the East. These included lobbying, participating in parades and meetings, supporting the party that endorsed woman suffrage, forming coalitions, and increasing the respectability of women's voting.[26] Campaigns in the West also benefited from eastern women who traveled west to organize suffrage support. Organizations sent observers to the West to determine the success or failure of women's enfranchisement.

This put to rest some of the arguments that claimed disaster if women regularly went to the polls. Although the population in the western states was small, they represented a steadily growing number of women voters. With women holding increasing political power, state and federal legislatures paid more attention to women's demands.

Women increasingly sought professions in the public sphere as more of them now had opportunities to attend college. Oberlin College in Ohio had opened its doors to Black men in 1835 and women in 1837, but for a long time it remained rare for either group to complete college degrees. New colleges, such as Vassar (1861), Wellesley (1881), and Bryn Mawr (1885) opened as women's institutions.[27] Even as critics of woman suffrage advocated for "true womanhood," the ideology based on women's role in the domestic sphere, people supported higher education for women.[28] But when the 1900 federal census showed that the birth rate for white women had dropped while immigrant women continued to have large families, some, including Theodore Roosevelt, argued that educated women who shirked their "duty" to procreate engaged in "race suicide."[29] Nevertheless, the ultimate success of suffrage would depend on the involvement and support of women (and men) of all of races, ethnicities, and classes.

Observers increasingly realized the illogic of the dire predictions of social disruption once expected of woman suffrage. And yet, some women actively resisted enfranchisement. Women opposed to woman suffrage published articles in lady's magazines; others frustrated suffragists by their indifference.[30] However, as more prominent people announced their support for suffrage, it prompted those who opposed it to acknowledge the need to organize. In 1890 a Massachusetts anti-suffrage organization began the journal *Remonstrance* to publicize the dangers of women in politics.[31] The anti-suffrage *Woman's Protest*, which eventually became the *Woman Patriot*, began in 1912 and continued until 1932.[32]

Ever ready to meet new challenges head on, suffrage leaders paid attention to anti-suffrage views and continued to revise their strategies to reach more people, including across class lines.[33] They published articles and books to express their arguments, disseminating them broadly. They held conventions and meetings regularly, seeking to educate women on their civic rights, political participation, and on how to speak before the public.[34] Suffragists also took to the road, traveling year-round to reach women and men in rural and urban areas. Activists toured the country in horse-drawn vehicles, then in automobiles, and they rode trolleys and trains as they spoke before large audiences. Local suffragists assisted with renting halls and lodging guest speakers. Many communities founded local clubs in response to these visits.

Suffragists established ever more sophisticated patterns of organization to reach voters. This was especially true in advance of a referendum, a question posed by legislators to the voters to decide if women could vote. Suffragists had success with referenda in Nebraska (1882), Colorado (1893), and California (1896). They also used telephones and telegraphs, marched in parades wearing clothing that evoked ideas of women as feminine and pure, and appropriated modern marketing techniques.[35] Influenced by consumer capitalism, suffragists designed and distributed buttons, pennants, ribbons, calendars, sheet music, fans, playing cards, toys, dolls, china dishes, and other souvenirs.[36] They mailed thousands of postcards, and they used yellow, a common suffrage color, for letters and promotional literature.[37] Suffragists spoke on street corners, organized motorcades and hikes, and held beautiful baby contests. They showed the electorate that women could be beautiful and domestic as they carried out their political

These suffragists, wearing suffrage sashes and riding under an umbrella that demands the vote for women, used a horse-drawn cart to reach people in rural areas. Only one of the women is identified, Laura Collins, and she is apparently from Steuben County, New York.

duties. Suffragists staged mock daring feats, such as rescuing an anti-suffragist who fell into the sea, or piloted planes while they scattered suffrage literature.[38] When the *Titanic* sank in 1912, suffragists, referring to rumors of men who wore women's coats to slip onto lifeboats, declared that women could not depend on men to protect them.[39] Anything that happened became fodder for suffrage publicity.

Having learned from the Civil War experience, suffragists knew better than to set aside their reform vision when the nation entered World War I. They used their political expertise to promote war preparedness and patriotism, sell Liberty Bonds, offer Red Cross service, and gather information for the government.[40] Others, however, refused to do war work, since their government denied them political equality. Peace activists opposed war entirely. Members of NAWSA, like Progressives and socialists, saw opportunities to demonstrate women's importance to the state in war work. Anti-suffragists, on the other hand, almost to a woman, devoted themselves to patriotic service and asked suffragists to put the campaign on hold.[41] Both suffragists and anti-suffragists portrayed themselves as ideal citizens, since citizenship required service to the state.

By the end of 1912, suffrage strategies changed again, influenced by Alice Paul's and Lucy Burns's involvement in NAWSA. Paul, inspired by her work with the radical branch of the British movement, became frustrated with what she saw as the stagnation of the US movement. Deeming the strategy of state-by-state campaigns ineffective, she and Lucy Burns took over NAWSA's Congressional Committee. From there, they focused on obtaining a federal amendment. As its first major event, the Congressional Committee held an enormous pageant and march in Washington, DC on the day before Woodrow Wilson's inauguration. Fifty African American women marched in the parade despite NAWSA leadership's attempt to marginalize them. The pageant drew national attention and, because many of the marchers suffered taunts and physical abuse from parade watchers, public sympathy. However, Catt accused Paul and Burns of defying the national leadership in their organizing and fundraising efforts, especially after they formed a concurrent affiliate group called the Congressional Union (CU). Paul and Burns soon left NAWSA and the Congressional Committee and ran the CU independently. The union, headquartered in Washington, DC, held daily meetings, established branches in different states, and published the

Suffragists established ever more sophisticated patterns of organization to reach voters.

"Just before a flight for the purpose of 'bombarding' the city with suffrage literature." Suffragists used the latest technologies and took advantage of all publicity opportunities as part of their efforts to spread the word about suffrage. In this photo, women plan to drop suffrage literature from an airplane. A December 3, 1916 article in the *New York Herald* describes their successful flight, although it ended in a Staten Island swamp.

the purpose of suffrage literature.

Suffragist, featuring articles by prominent authors. In 1916, the Congressional Union established the National Woman's Party.

Holding the political party in power responsible for women's disenfranchisement, as well as highlighting the hypocrisy of "fighting for democracy abroad," a phrase Wilson often repeated, members of the National Woman's Party picketed the White House from 1917 to early 1919. Critics resented the women picketing a war-time president. As a result, authorities arrested some 500 women, and as many as 170 suffered imprisonment and forced feeding.[42] Yet, women from all over the United States traveled to Washington to take their places on the picket lines. Because both groups vied for membership and media attention as they worked for the same goal,

MR. PRESIDENT WHAT WILL YOU DO FOR WOMAN SUFFRAGE

their competing strategies won greater overall support for woman suffrage.

During these same years, NAWSA president Carrie Chapman Catt implemented her "winning plan." In it, she advocated for state enfranchisement as well as a federal amendment. By 1917 women had won the vote in eleven western states.[43] After New York voters approved a woman suffrage referendum, suffragists shifted their focus to Congress and a federal constitutional amendment. Persuaded by suffrage arguments, some congressmen claimed that enfranchising women should be a war measure. Wilson, surely moved by the determination of the militant suffragists, increased suffrage agitation, and widening support from politicians, finally declared he would back a federal amendment. It still

Hundreds of National Woman's Party members from all over the United States came to Washington to picket the White House, despite the risk of arrest and prison terms. This image shows College Day in the picket line. Suffragists sought to highlight the status of members whenever possible.

The suffrage movement represents an extraordinary effort on the part of women to change not only their role in the polity, but also the perception of women as engaged civic-minded citizens.

took several votes, however, before both the House of Representatives and the Senate passed the measure.

Once passed, the amendment required ratification by at least thirty-six states. Suffragists and anti-suffragists campaigned vigorously. They gathered wherever a state legislature convened to debate the amendment, speaking directly with legislators. They sent a flurry of telegrams to press their views, and each side kept a tally of states as legislatures voted on the amendment. Tennessee ("Armageddon," to suffragists) became the last state to ratify the amendment and did so by a single vote. Secretary of State Bainbridge Colby signed the certificate of ratification for the Nineteenth Amendment to the Constitution on August 26, 1920. No suffragists were present when he signed it.[44]

The suffrage movement represents an extraordinary effort on the part of women to change not only their role in the polity, but also the perception of women as engaged civic-minded citizens. Never again would women, as a class of citizens, be content with lives defined by domesticity. Although the process had been long and complicated, and the movement steeped in conflict and controversy, suffragists used ever more effective strategies that ultimately won them the right to full political participation.

The author would like to thank two anonymous reviewers and members of the Rochester United States History Draft group, including Alison Parker, Tamar Carroll, Timothy Kneeland, Michael Brown, Suzanne Schnittman, and Jenny Lloyd, for comments.

Abby Kelley

Abby Kelley was an abolitionist (someone opposed to slavery) and an early women's rights advocate. Devoting her life to creating a more equitable society, she used her skills as a lecturer and educator to advocate for the rights of African Americans and women.

Kelley was born in Massachusetts in 1811. Her Quaker upbringing influenced her outlook on life. In addition to opposing slavery, many Quakers also believed in equal educational opportunities for men and women. As a result, Abby received an advanced education, including instruction in spelling, grammar, botany, and astronomy. After attending school, she became an educator. While teaching in Lynn, MA, Kelley developed into a staunch abolitionist by reading William Lloyd Garrison's newspaper *The Liberator*.

In 1838, Kelley made her first public speech at an anti-slavery convention in Philadelphia. At the time, it was unusual for a woman to speak in public, let alone address a crowd of male onlookers. Her speeches were so effective, that she became a highly sought-out lecturer. She traveled throughout New England talking about the horrors of slavery.

Kelley decided to become a reformer, but she did not concentrate solely on abolition. She also voiced the importance of equal rights for African Americans and women, issues that people like Elizabeth Cady Stanton and Susan B. Anthony also supported.

In 1845, Kelley married fellow abolitionist Stephen Symonds Foster. The couple became known for their rousing and inspiring speeches. They decided to settle in Massachusetts and make a permanent home. The couple purchased Liberty Farm in 1847 and devoted their lives to helping enslaved men and women fleeing bondage. They used their home to hide enslaved individuals fleeing north on the Underground Railroad. Today, Liberty Farm is a National Historic Landmark.

After the Civil War, Kelley devoted her energy to fighting for equal rights and women's suffrage. Against the wishes of many woman suffragists, Abby Kelley Foster supported the Fifteenth Amendment. Ratified in 1870, the amendment

recognized Black men's voting rights. Kelley believed in furthering the rights of African American men, even if the amendment did not include voting rights for women.

In her later years, Abbey Kelley was unable to travel and give lectures. Despite her age, she continued to advocate for women's rights. Kelley did not have the right to vote on how her tax money was spent, and she refused to pay property taxes as a form of protest. As a result, her property was auctioned off by the state several times. Her friends, however, repeatedly purchased the house and gifted Liberty Farm back to Kelley.

Abbey Kelley continued to fight for the rights of marginalized communities until her death in 1887.

Associated Places:
Liberty Farm, Worcester, Massachusetts (listed on the National Register of Historic Places and designated a National Historic Landmark).

—Katherine Crawford-Lackey

Anti-Suffragism in the United States

by Rebecca A. Rix

From the 1840s, when six New York women protested taxation without representation, through the 1920s, after ratification of the Nineteenth Amendment, supporters of women's right to vote met opposition.[1] In the early nineteenth century, suffragists were among the radical reformers threatening to democratize a republic still based on status hierarchies. After the Civil War and Reconstruction emancipated enslaved African Americans, established birthright citizenship, and promised equal protection to all citizens, suffragists and reformers fought for decades to realize that equality. Anti-suffragists, conversely, fought to maintain the male-headed family, rather than the individual citizen, as the representative unit of republican government.[2]

For anti-suffragists, the franchise meant more than just the right to enter a voting booth and cast a ballot. The vote for them was an affirmation of the fundamental political equality of all persons holding it, in both the private and public spheres. This was a radical interpretation of the founding ideals that anti-suffragists were eager to extinguish wherever it threatened the republic.

While anti-suffragists eventually lost their battle, their opposition delayed woman suffrage for decades. They also transformed family-based republicanism from a patrician opposition to democratization into a popular defense of tradition and family against feminism and the social welfare state. Suffragists' belief in individual

family, but also states' rights and "local self government." This was a polite term that connoted government by propertied white men, regardless of African American federal citizenship rights.[15] As Alabama Senator John Tyler Morgan explained, a woman suffrage amendment would draw a "line of political demarcation through a man's household." It would, he argued, "open to the intrusion of politics and politicians that sacred circle of the family where no man should be permitted to intrude."[16]

In defending local self-government, anti-suffragists evoked memories of federal troops supervising southern polls and the alliance of abolitionists and suffragists. While they warned against federal interference with southern Jim Crow laws, they also appealed to northerners leading their own antidemocratic movements.[17] By the mid-1880s, congressional Democrats' success in stalling legislation and northern anti-suffragists' remonstrances led to the suffrage movement's congressional "doldrums."[18]

Suffragists had some successes at the state level as Reconstruction ended. This provoked anti-suffragists to organize, first in Massachusetts and then in other states. When, in 1882, the American Woman Suffrage Association (AWSA) sought to expand on an 1879 Massachusetts partial woman suffrage measure, Massachusetts anti-suffragists organized to counter the considerable influence of celebrated abolitionist-suffragists such as Lucy Stone and Julia Ward Howe. As anti-suffragist Mrs. Charles Eliot Guild recalled, it was a moment when conservative women—whose postbellum political reputation was tarnished by their families' non-abolitionism—claimed their "right to be heard" as remonstrants.[19] The first remonstrants operated within a patrician social network of Massachusetts's founding families. They were represented by prominent male relatives, including State Senator George Crocker, who advised them on legislative developments; publisher Henry Houghton, who printed anti-suffrage publications; and Harvard historian and critic of universal manhood suffrage, Francis Parkman.[20] Parkman added his *Some of the Reasons against Woman Suffrage* to a growing anti-suffrage literature that defended the traditional, historical, political, and evolutionary wisdom of men's and women's complementary, distinct forms of citizenship.[21] The AWSA's Massachusetts activity kept the remonstrants busy through the 1880s. The growing suffrage movement in other states also engaged Massachusetts anti-suffragists beyond their state borders. Indeed, it was South Dakota's 1890 woman suffrage referendum that inspired the transformation of their local bulletin into a nationally distributed publication, *The Remonstrance*.[22]

As Alabama Senator John Tyler Morgan explained, a woman suffrage amendment would draw a "line of political demarcation through a man's household."

Massachusetts remonstrants corresponded with Chicago's Caroline Corbin, a descendent of old northeastern families, who had moved west with her enterprising merchant husband.[23] Chicago was a railroad hub between western mines, forests, and farms and eastern capital and goods. Its rapid urbanization, industrialization, and expanding immigrant population gave rise to pressing social problems. Whereas Massachusetts anti-suffragists faced former abolitionist suffragists, Corbin contended with progressive reformers like Jane Addams. Addams viewed the western city as an opportunity for female and male reformers to study social problems and experiment with social reform. Addams's Hull House offered intellectual community and a laboratory for municipal reformers, useful social and educational programs for local workers and immigrants, and a professional network for female social scientists and reformers.[24]

Addams and Corbin held opposing views of how to ameliorate the social and economic misery of the 1890s generally, and of Chicago specifically. For Addams, woman suffrage was essential to governing a modern urban, industrial, and multiethnic society. Real democracy required developing individual citizens' capacities, prioritizing the public good, and regulating the corrupting influences of poverty, disease, greed, and machine politics. For Addams, woman suffrage promised to clean up politics and fuel reform as women joined men in analyzing and experimenting with socialism, labor unionism, and other reform movements. For Corbin, reform experimentation and woman suffrage were anathema to progress, because both threatened the very foundations of social order. Restricting suffrage to male heads of household at once ennobled men and obliged them to support families and serve their community. Virtual representation reflected a wise public policy based on human evolution—marked by highly differentiated gender roles—and the progress of civilization. Family unity was the foundation of organic social unity. Enfranchising women would fuel individual aspirations to equality, which would lead to socialism.[25]

Suffragists formed many important local and national political alliances in the 1890s, lending credence to Corbin's warnings to eastern antis. Colorado's successful 1893 suffrage referendum reflected an alliance between western suffragists and

These anti-suffrage campaign pins would have been distributed at anti-suffrage organization storefronts, along with pamphlets, postcards, and signs.

Populists, supported by farmers and labor. As suffrage-reform alliances threatened to a democratic revolt in the states, remonstrants founded three important state anti-suffrage organizations.[26] The seasoned Massachusetts remonstrants helped New York remonstrants defeat an attempt to add woman suffrage to the state constitution in 1894. The threat led New York women to organize the first formal state anti-suffrage organization.[27] Their New York Association Opposed to Woman Suffrage (NYAOWS) provided a model adopted by Massachusetts (Massachusetts Association Opposed to the Further Extension of Suffrage to Women [MAOFESW], 1895) and Illinois (Illinois Association Opposed to Woman Suffrage [IAOWS], 1897). These state organizations cooperated with each other and with male anti-suffragists, who provided them legal and political advice.

Women anti-suffragists appeared for each legislative battle to disprove suffragists' claim to speak for all women. NYAOWS and MAOFESW leaders organized new state anti-suffrage associations and distributed anti-suffrage literature and association newspapers as far away as Oregon, Washington, California, Iowa, and other endangered states. In 1911, they formed the National Association Opposed to Woman Suffrage (NAOWS), led by NYAOWS president Josephine Dodge. NAOWS launched a new national publication, the *Woman's Protest*. Most western (and later, southern) state associations were founded by wealthy white women linked to NAOWS members by social networks.[28] Their task was to legitimate family-based suffrage and its political analog, local self-government by propertied elites, to voters with increasingly democratic aspirations. Antisuffragists carried out public education campaigns by distributing campaign buttons through social networks and storefront headquarters. They appealed to working-men's and businessmen's economic interests and desires to protect their families and communities against feminism, Progressivism, populism, and socialism. In the early twentieth century, anti-suffragists had to counter suffragists' allegations that "Antis" were selfish aristocrats or, worse,

New York Senate Republican leader John Raines and his Democratic counterpart, "Tom" Grady, receive anti-suffragists' petitions in this 1907 *Harpers Weekly* cover. Anti-suffragists prevailed until 1917, when New York joined the many states that enfranchised women prior to the Nineteenth Amendment.

"O SAVE US, SENATORS, FROM OURSELVES!"

Women were active in these areas of reform, and women's political power influenced the 1912 presidential election.

that they provided political cover for immoral "interests" who benefitted from reform-minded women's disfranchisement.

While the Populist Party disintegrated after the 1896 election, its reforms, personnel, and democratic ideology continued to gain popularity. The Populists' 1892 and 1896 platforms united reformers against monopolistic trusts, political corruption, vice, and the exploitation of workers and small businesses. The Democratic Party absorbed many Populists. In the solidly Democratic South, they had to acquiesce to suffrage restrictions as Jim Crow solidified.[29] In the West, however, Populist reformers joined Progressives and played Democrats against Republicans, using new tools for direct lawmaking. The ballot initiative enabled reformers to write laws for approval by voters, instead of filtering popular sovereignty through legislators. Referenda and recalls provided accountability. Colorado was first among many western states to enfranchise women this way. Western anti-suffragists, often drawn from commercial cities' founding families, conferred with eastern anti-suffragists to defend against these blows at "representative government."[30] Anti-suffragists' defense of property rights and virtual representation had long been consonant with regionally distinct forms of local self-government. This became politically problematic amid growing debates over using federal power to enact needed reforms, including woman suffrage, regulating monopolistic trusts, regulating liquor consumption, adjudicating labor conflicts, and protecting African Americans' rights.

Women were active in all these areas of reform, and women's political power influenced the 1912 presidential election. The four presidential candidates faced a new constituency in western states—newly enfranchised women. Progressive Theodore Roosevelt and Socialist Eugene Debs endorsed woman suffrage.[31] Two new Populist-Progressive constitutional amendments (the Sixteenth, income tax, and the Seventeenth, direct election of senators) inspired suffragists and Prohibitionists, who had long advocated for woman suffrage.[32] While intrinsically important, a number of reformers also viewed woman suffrage as an expedient to those promoting child welfare, Prohibition, labor regulation, unionism, African American civil rights, and many other reforms. Indeed, as suffragists championed Progressive reforms, many portrayed "Antis" as witless wealthy women associated with corrupt and corrupting interests.

Yet many anti-suffragists were also devoted reformers. Among their anti-equality arguments were those for preserving state gender-based protective labor legislation. NAOWS's Minnie Bronson, a Theodore Roosevelt administration veteran, invoked her expertise in labor law to observe that political equality threatened women's labor laws. As "feminism" emerged in the 1910s, anti-suffragists argued that educated, affluent women might benefit from gender equality. But what of workingwomen who benefitted from labor legislation premised on the state's interest in protecting women's maternal health?[33] Against arguments that the vote would enhance workingwomen's ability to win labor legislation, Bronson maintained that women's political equality might preclude state protective labor legislation that was constitutional only because women were, presumably, the weaker sex.[34]

The conflict between a federal woman suffrage amendment and paternalistic protection also threatened Jim Crow and southern traditions, southern anti-suffragists warned with increasing alarm in the 1910s. Southern antis feared that the "Anthony Amendment," like the Fifteenth Amendment, would bring federal scrutiny of state polls, the enfranchisement of southern female Progressives, and growth of the Black middle class.[35] The Fifteenth Amendment had languished under Jim Crow for decades. But in 1915 the new National Association for the Advancement of Colored People won its Supreme Court case against grandfather clauses that exempted some (white) voters from voting restrictions based on the status of their ancestors.[36] During World War I, National American Woman Suffrage Association president Carrie Chapman Catt argued in a special suffrage issue of W. E. B. Du Bois's the *Crisis*, that Wilson's wartime democratic ideals required universal enfranchisement regardless of sex, race, or ethnicity.[37] With local Progressives for Prohibition and child labor regulation, and a national enthusiasm for Progressivism, southern anti-suffragists continued to invoke familiar tropes of federal interference in "local" affairs. This halted the nascent suffrage movement in the region.

When Congress sent the Nineteenth Amendment to the states in 1919, the NAOWS counted the southern states critical among the thirteen states required to stymie its ratification. Confident in the conservatism of northeastern and southern states, they were dismayed when Tennessee became the thirty-sixth and final needed state to ratify the amendment in 1920.

After ratification, anti-suffrage leaders responded in different ways. While some former anti-suffragists refused to vote, many realized that their votes were necessary to counter what many Americans viewed as a powerful, Progressive women's bloc. In North Carolina, May Hilliard Hinton, the president of the state's Rejection

As "feminism" emerged in the 1910s, anti-suffragists argued that educated, affluent women might benefit from gender equality. But what of workingwomen who benefitted from labor legislation premised on the state's interest in protecting women's maternal health?

In battles against suffragists and their allies during Reconstruction and afterward, opposing those who saw in federal citizenship a means of realizing government by, for, and of the people, anti-suffragists developed a competing, conservative vision.

(anti-ratification) League, appealed to the state's (white) women to register and vote, as did the governor's anti-suffrage wife.[38] Many northern anti-suffrage leaders entered partisan politics following the lead of New York anti-suffragists who had made use of their voting power since 1917 to oppose woman suffrage and Progressivism.[39] After ratification, northeastern anti-suffrage leaders organized within the Republican Party, contributing to its rightward shift in the 1920s. Elizabeth Lowell Putnam, MAOFESW leader and sister of Harvard president A. Lawrence Lowell, worked against Progressive Republicans as vice president of the Republican Club of Massachusetts. She was the first woman elected president of the Massachusetts Electoral College. An advocate of maternal and children's social reforms who once supported the fledgling US Children's Bureau, Putnam became opposed to its Progressive leadership and the Harding-era expansion of federal social welfare programs and the popular federal child labor amendment.[40] Putnam, like Harriet Frothingham of the Woman Patriots' and their male allies in the Sentinels of the Republic and the Liberty League, opposed a national social welfare state as socialistic. They challenged the Nineteenth Amendment's constitutionality and also Congress's use of its taxing power for a joint federal-state maternal and infancy welfare program. They lost both cases before the US Supreme Court.[41] In 1924, these Massachusetts-based groups joined with conservative Catholics and others to organize Massachusetts voters against state ratification of the popular Child Labor Amendment to the US Constitution. They argued that enabling Congress to regulate child labor amounted to the "nationalization" of children. While reformers viewed children's health and education programs as promoting the growth of young citizens' individual capacities for common good, conservatives viewed them as a threat to family, tradition, religion, and local self-government. As anti-suffragists had long done, they insisted instead on the protection of men's traditional rights, expounding a democratized and modernized vision of family-based liberty.[42]

For fifty years, anti-suffragists were a force in US political life. In battles against suffragists and their allies during Reconstruction and afterward, opposing those who saw in federal citizenship a means of realizing government by, for, and of the people, anti-suffragists developed a competing, conservative vision. Initially defending the traditional prerogatives of property and patriarchy, by the mid-1920s they shed the exclusivity and elitism of that vision to make anti-Progressivism appealing to a conservative working-class and middle-class electorate, including women, whose votes they had once opposed.

The Statue of Liberty is an international symbol of freedom and democracy, and it is also a site of protest. The act of using the statue as a platform for protest began at its unveiling on October 28, 1886.

The statue was a gift to the United States from France, signifying the friendship between the two nations. As the city of New York prepared to celebrate the dedication of the statue, the New York City Woman Suffrage Association (NYCWSA) voiced its discontent. Leaders of the organization, including Lillie Devereux Blake and Matilda Joslyn Gage, were unhappy with the statue's form. Gage declared that "to make the Statue of Liberty a woman was simply setting up a gigantic lie in the gaze of nations."[1] The statue, made in the form of a woman, represented American liberty. Gage felt that the statue mocked American women, who still lacked many rights and privileges. Wanting to have a presence at the unveiling ceremony, Blake and the NYCWSA petitioned ceremony planners for entrance. Their request was denied, yet the women refused to be excluded.

On the day of the ceremony, a dense fog hung over New York Harbor. As American and French delegates gathered on Liberty Island for the unveiling ceremony, the sun dissipated the dreary weather. With the sky clear, the 305-foot tall Lady Liberty visibly towered over onlookers. Ceremony

Modern photo of the upper half of Lady Liberty.

festivities included speeches by politicians, music and signal guns, and a water parade. As participants boarded boats to parade through the harbor, they were confronted by local suffragists.

Refusing to be excluded from the festivities, Blake and the NYCWSA used the last of their funds to rent a steamer. The New York City suffragists joined the water parade, waving banners of protest at American and French delegates. While their presence caused little disruption, the women changed the way suffragists voiced their frustration. Instead of using old tactics such as making speeches or lobbying politicians, the women used direct confrontation as a form of protest. Using the Statue of Liberty as a focal point, the suffragists set a precedent for future demonstrations.

Face of Lady Liberty waiting to be installed.

Lady Liberty in Paris workshop, not yet assembled.

Associated Places:
Statue of Liberty National Monument, Ellis Island, New York and New Jersey.

—Katherine Crawford-Lackey

African American Women and the Nineteenth Amendment

by Sharon Harley

African American women, though often overlooked in the history of woman suffrage, engaged in significant reform efforts and political activism leading to and following the ratification in 1920 of the Nineteenth Amendment. This amendment barred states from denying American women the right to vote on the basis of their sex. They had as much—or more—at stake in the struggle as white women. From the earliest years of the suffrage movement, Black women worked side by side with white suffragists. By the late nineteenth century, however, the suffrage movement splintered over the issue of race in the years after the Civil War. In response, Black women formed their own organizations to continue their efforts to secure and protect the rights of all women, and men.

The US women's rights movement was closely allied with the antislavery movement. Before the Civil War, Black and white abolitionists and suffragists joined together in common cause. During the antebellum period, a small cohort of formerly enslaved and free Black women were active in women's rights circles. Sojourner Truth, Harriet Tubman, Maria W. Stewart, Henrietta Purvis, Harriet Forten Purvis, Sarah Remond, and Mary Ann Shadd Cary were all active in women's rights circles. They were joined in their advocacy of women's rights and suffrage by prominent Black men, including Frederick Douglass, Charles Lenox Remond, and Robert Purvis. Together, they worked in collaboration with white abolitionists and women's rights activists, including William Lloyd Garrison, Elizabeth Cady Stanton, and Susan B. Anthony.[1]

Following the 1848 women's rights convention in Seneca Falls, New York, prominent free Black women abolitionists and suffragists attended, spoke, and assumed leadership positions at multiple women's rights gatherings throughout the 1850s and 1860s. In 1851, former slave Sojourner Truth delivered her famous "Ain't I a Woman" speech at the national women's rights convention in Akron, Ohio. Sarah Remond and her brother Charles won wide acclaim for their pro-woman suffrage speeches at the 1858 National Woman's Rights Convention in New York City.[2]

With the end of the Civil War, arguments for woman suffrage became entwined with debates over the rights of former slaves and the meaning of citizenship. Sisters Margaretta Forten and Harriet Forten Purvis helped to establish the interracial Philadelphia Suffrage Association in 1866. They and other Black women were active in the new American Equal Rights Association (AERA), an organization formed by former abolitionists and women's rights advocates. The organization endorsed both women's and Black men's right to vote. Purvis served on the AERA executive committee. Abolitionist Frances Ellen Watkins Harper spoke on behalf of woman suffrage at the founding meeting of the AERA; Sojourner Truth gave a major address at its first anniversary meeting.[3]

But with the proposal of the Fifteenth Amendment, which would enfranchise Black men but not women, interracial and mixed-gender coalitions began to deteriorate. Suffragists had to choose between insisting on universal rights or accepting the priority of Black male suffrage. The split in the suffrage movement over the Fifteenth Amendment prompted Elizabeth Cady Stanton and Susan B. Anthony to sever ties with the AERA. Together they formed the National Woman Suffrage Association (NWSA), which promoted universal suffrage. The NWSA insisted that Black men should not receive the vote before white women. Stanton and Anthony's racist remarks about Black men evoked intense anger on the part of Black suffragists, including long-time allies Frederick Douglass and Frances Ellen Watkins Harper. As a result, Harper supported the Fifteenth Amendment. This was despite her being a fiercely independent woman who believed women were equal, indeed, superior to men in their level of productivity. In her mind, men were talkers, while women were doers.[4] Harper joined the new American Woman Suffrage Association (AWSA). The AWSA supported both Black suffrage and

Frances E. W. Harper, ca. 1898.

woman suffrage and took a state-by-state approach to securing women's right to vote. As Harper proclaimed in her closing remarks at the 1873 AWSA convention, "much as white women need the ballot, colored women need it more."[5] Many whites, including some white female suffragists, publicly denounced Black male suffrage. Black women, on the other hand, incorporated Black male suffrage as an important component of their suffrage goals.

Black women, however, did become members of both the Stanton and Anthony-led NWSA and the Lucy Stone and Julia Ward Howe-led AWSA. Hattie Purvis was a delegate to the NWSA (as well as a member of the executive committee of the Pennsylvania State Suffrage Association). Among the prominent African American reformers and suffragists who joined the AWSA were Charlotte Forten and Josephine St. Pierre Ruffin. St. Pierre Ruffin was also a member of the Massachusetts Woman Suffrage Association.[6]

Black women attended and spoke out at political and religious meetings and public rallies. Their enthusiasm and political engagement within and outside suffrage campaigns was particularly concerning to whites in the post-emancipation South.

Black women attended and spoke out at political and religious meetings and public rallies. Their enthusiasm and political engagement within and outside suffrage campaigns was particularly concerning to whites in the post-emancipation South.[7] The suffrage work of Charlotte ("Lottie") Rollin shows the long history of African American women's political activism outside the Northeast and beyond women's rights conferences and organizations. In 1866, a year before chairing the inaugural meeting of the South Carolina Woman's Rights Association, Rollin courageously proclaimed her support for universal suffrage at a meeting of the South Carolina House of Representatives. In 1870, she was the elected secretary of the South Carolina Woman's Rights Association, an affiliate of the AWSA. Rollin, along with her sisters Frances and Louisa and other local women, figured prominently in Reconstruction politics and woman suffrage campaigns at the local and national levels in the early 1870s. South Carolina's African American woman suffrage advocates were encouraged by African American men. In certain 1870 South Carolina district elections, Black election officials encouraged Black women to vote. This was an action the Rollins sisters and some other African American women were already assuming (or attempting) on their own.[8] In 1871, pioneer suffragist, newspaper editor, and first female law school student at Howard University Mary Ann Shadd Cary, with several other women, attempted, unsuccessfully, to register to vote in Washington, DC. This failure notwithstanding, they insisted upon and secured an official signed affidavit recognizing that they had attempted to vote.[9]

Like white suffragists, African American women linked suffrage to a multitude of political and economic issues in order to further their cause. They engaged in multiple strategies to secure women's political and voting rights within and outside the organized suffrage movement. At the same time, they combatted anti-Black discrimination in the southern United States and within the predominantly white national woman suffrage organizations.

Over time, tensions between Stanton, Anthony, and Douglass subsided. The discrimination against Black women in the woman suffrage movement continued as certain white woman suffragist leaders sought southern white male and female support. The anti-Black rhetoric and actions of NWSA leaders Susan B. Anthony and Elizabeth Cady Stanton persisted. But so did African American women's courageous battles for both gender and racial equality. In 1876, Cary wrote to leaders of the National Woman Suffrage Association. She urged them to place the names of ninety-four Washington, DC, Black woman suffragists on their Declaration of the Rights of the Women of the United States. This Declaration was to be issued on the one-hundredth anniversary of American Independence. It concluded, "we ask justice, we ask equality, we ask that all the civil and political rights that belong to citizens of the United States, be guaranteed to us and our daughters forever." While unsuccessful in having their names added, Cary remained a committed suffrage activist, speaking at the 1878 NWSA meeting. Two years later, she formed the Colored Woman's Franchise Association in Washington, DC. This organization linked suffrage not just to political rights but to education and labor issues.[10]

Late nineteenth-century Black women believed there was an inextricable link between effective reform work and women's right to vote. Many Black suffragists were active in the temperance movement, including Hattie Purvis, Frances Ellen Watkins Harper, and Gertrude Bustill Mossell. Purvis and Harper served as Superintendent of Work among Colored People in the Woman's Christian Temperance Union. Purvis also served, from 1883 to 1900, as a delegate to the National Woman Suffrage Association. Mossell wrote pro-suffrage articles for the Black press. In her 1881 article, "Woman's Suffrage," reprinted in an 1885 issue of *New York Freeman*, Mossell urged readers to become more knowledgeable about suffrage history and women's rights. Purvis, Harper, Mossell, and other Black woman suffragists and reformers argued that intemperance was a major obstacle to racial advancement. The passage of federal woman suffrage would, they said, significantly reduce this and other social ills.[11]

Despite all this important work by Black suffragists, the mainstream suffrage movement continued its

Like white suffragists, African American women linked suffrage to a multitude of political and economic issues in order to further their cause. They engaged in multiple strategies to secure women's political and voting rights within and outside the organized suffrage movement.

racially discriminatory practices. It even condoned white supremacist ideologies to garner southern support for white women's voting rights. Consequently, African American women and men became increasingly marginalized and discriminated against at woman suffrage meetings, campaigns, and marches.[12] Even after the NWSA and the AWSA reconciled to form the National American Woman Suffrage Association (NAWSA) in 1890, Anthony and other white suffragists in the South and the North continued to choose expediency over loyalty and justice when it came to Black suffragists. In 1895, Anthony asked her "friend" and veteran woman suffrage supporter Frederick Douglass not to attend the upcoming NAWSA convention in Atlanta. As she later explained to Ida B. Wells-Barnett, Douglass's presence on the stage with the honored guests would have offended the southern hosts. Wells-Barnett and other suffragists reprimanded Anthony and other white women activists for giving in to racial prejudice. During the 1903 NAWSA meeting in New Orleans, the *Times Democrat* denounced the organization's anti-Black states' rights strategy. It had, they argued, a negative impact on Black women's quest for suffrage.[13]

There were exceptions to the discriminatory traditions among suffragists. In New England, Josephine St. Pierre Ruffin claimed she had been warmly welcomed by Lucy Stone, Julia Ward Howe, and others. Some African American women, such as internationally prominent women's rights activists and speaker Mary Church Terrell, belonged to and participated in NAWSA meetings and activities. This in spite of the fact the new organization discriminated against them to woo southern and white male support for woman suffrage.

Facing page: Mary Church Terrell, ca. 1890.

In the closing decades of the nineteenth century more Black women formed their own local and regional woman suffrage clubs. In 1896, the National Association of Colored Women (NACW) was established. The NACW, which elected Terrell as it first national president, provided Black women a national platform to advocate for woman suffrage and women's rights causes. From the organization's inception and throughout the twentieth century, Terrell, Ruffin, Barrier Williams, Wells-Barnett, and numerous NACW members and leaders fought for woman suffrage. They shared their pro-suffrage sentiments and activities at regional and national NACW conventions and in the white and Black press.

Despite the discrimination Black women experienced, including the rejection of Josephine St. Pierre Ruffin's effort to represent the NACW in the General

Ida B. Wells, ca. 1891.

Federation of Women's Clubs, Black women cautiously joined interracial efforts to secure the ballot for women. They also worked to expand women's engagement in electoral politics as canvassers, organizers, and voters. Prominent anti-lynching activist, NACW member, and suffragist Ida B. Wells-Barnett organized, in 1913, the first Black woman suffrage club in Illinois, the Chicago-based Alpha Suffrage Club. She and other midwestern women participated in nonpartisan NACW, NAWSA, and Alpha Club campaigns and political rallies. Most Black women, however, also supported Republican Party platforms and candidates.[14]

As the suffrage movement moved into its final phase in the early decades of the twentieth century, local and national white woman suffrage organizations claimed racial inclusivity. And they did have African American women as active members. But the actions and policy statements of their leaders reflected a very different racial reality—one that worsened over time. When Alice Paul, founder of the National Woman's Party, organized a woman suffrage parade in 1913, scheduled a day before the inauguration of Woodrow Wilson, the first US president from the South, her accommodating acquiescence to white racism typified the worsening racial climate within the suffrage movement. Prior to the parade, Wells-Barnett, representing the Alpha Suffrage Club, was asked to march at the rear of the parade rather than with the white Chicago delegation. In keeping with her resistant and radical personality, Wells-Barnett refused to join her fellow Black suffragists at the rear. Instead, as the all-white Chicago delegation passed, Wells-Barnett emerged from the crowd and entered the line between two white Chicago women and marched and with them, as she knew to be just.[15]

NACW founder Mary Church Terrell, however, marched with the all-Black delegation. Terrell later told Walter White, of the National Association for the Advancement of Colored People (NAACP), in denouncing the anti-Black stance of Paul and other white woman suffrage leaders, that she believed if white suffrage leaders, including Paul, could pass the amendment without giving Black women the vote, they would. This was a claim Paul and other white suffragists denied while persisting in organizing white women exclusively in various southern states.[16] The opposition African American women faced was the subject of NACW and NAACP leader Mary B. Talbert's 1915 *Crisis* article, "Women and Colored Women." As Talbert pointed out, "with us as colored women, this struggle becomes two-fold, first, because we are women and second, because we are colored women."[17]

Talbert's essay was one of several by a small cadre of Black female and male intellectuals and public figures who had participated in a symposium on "Votes for Women." Their remarks appeared in the August 1915 issue of the *Crisis*, the national organ of the NAACP. In her essay, Black feminist leader and educator Nannie Helen Burroughs offered a cryptic but profound response to a white woman's query about what Black women would do with the ballot. "What can she do without it?" she retorted. Expressing a common line of thinking, Burroughs and other Black women political activists proclaimed that the Black woman "needs the ballot, to reckon with men who place no value upon her virtue, and to mould [*sic*] healthy sentiment in favor of her own protection."[18] Burroughs echoed an idea previously expressed by Adella Hunt Logan, a life member of the National American Woman Suffrage Association and active member of the Tuskegee Woman's Club, in an earlier monthly Black publication, *Colored American Magazine*:

> *If white American women, with all their natural and acquired advantages, need the ballot, that right protective of all other rights; if Anglo Saxons have been helped by it . . . how much more do black Americans, male and female need the strong defense of a vote to help secure them their right to life, liberty and the pursuit of happiness?*[19]

Mary B. Talbert, ca. 1901.

*An examination
of Black women's
post-1920 political
life reveals that
rather than ending,
the Nineteenth
Amendment
was a starting
point for African
American women's
involvement in
electoral politics in
the years to come.*

These arguments notwithstanding, on the eve of ratification of the Nineteenth Amendment, white suffragists, fearing offending white southerners, continued their racially discriminatory practices toward Black suffragists. In 1919, NAWSA president Carrie Chapman Catt opposed admitting the Northeastern Federation of Women's Clubs, a regional body of Black clubwomen, as a member of the national suffrage organization out of fear of offending white voters. When at last the Nineteenth Amendment was ratified, African American women voters in the Jim Crow South encountered the very same disfranchisement strategies and anti-Black violence that led to the disfranchisement of Black men. Thus, Black women had to continue their fight to secure voting privileges, for both men and women.

Racism and discrimination within and outside organized woman suffrage campaigns and anti-Black racial violence forced Black women early on to link their right to vote to the restoration of Black male suffrage and civil rights activism. African American suffragist and radical activist Angelina Weld Grimké, named for her great aunt, suffragist Angelina Grimké Weld, boldly and optimistically asserted, "injustices will end" between the sexes when woman "gains the ballot."[20] But instead, the struggle continued.

Black women's political engagement from the antebellum period to the opening decades of the twentieth century helped to define their post-1920 political activism. Following ratification of the Nineteenth Amendment, the battle for the vote ended for white women. For African American women the outcome was less clear. Hoping to combat post–World War I anti-Black racial violence and the disfranchisement of Black men, particularly in the South, Black women's engagement in electoral politics and radical activism continued. In fact, it expanded after ratification. An examination of Black women's post-1920 political life reveals that rather than ending, the Nineteenth Amendment was a starting point for African American women's involvement in electoral politics in the years to come.[21] Indeed, Oscar De Priest credited Black women with being the deciding factor in his election in 1928. He was the first African American elected to the United States House of Representatives since Reconstruction.[22] Woman suffrage struggles in the United States were one part of a long and impressive history of African American women's political engagement to promote women's rights and to share equally in the advancement of the race.

Nannie Helen Burroughs

Born in Orange, Virginia in 1879, Nannie Helen Burroughs was the descendant of enslaved individuals. Her father died when she was young and her widowed mother relocated the family to Washington, DC.

Burroughs attended the M Street High School in Washington. Now a community center, this building was the one of the first high schools for African Americans in the United States. She studied under noted suffragist and early civil rights advocate Mary Church Terrell. Burroughs graduated with honors in 1896.

Despite her academic achievements, Burroughs was turned down for a Washington DC public school teaching position. Undeterred, Burroughs spent the next decade attending college and working for the National Baptist Convention (NBC).

In the early 1900s, Burroughs asked the NBC for funds to open her own school to educate and train working-class African American women. To support her cause, the organization purchased six acres of land in Northeast Washington, DC Burroughs then needed money to construct the school. She did not, however, have unanimous support. Early civil rights leader Booker T. Washington did not believe African Americans would donate money for the school.

But Burroughs did not want to rely on money from wealthy white donors. Relying on small denotations from African American women and children from the community, Burroughs managed to raise enough money to open the National Training School for Women and Girls in 1909. The school taught Black women both practical and professional skills.

Even though some people disagreed with teaching women skills other than domestic work, the school was popular in the first half of the twentieth century. The school originally operated out of a small farm house. In 1928, a larger building named Trades Hall was constructed. The hall housed twelve classrooms, three offices, an assembly area, and a print shop.

In addition to founding the National Training School for Women and Girls, Burroughs also advocated for greater civil rights for African Americans and women. At the time, Black women had few career choices. Many did domestic work like cooking and cleaning. Burroughs believed women should have the opportunity to receive an education and job training. She wrote about the need for Black and white women to work together to achieve the right to vote. She believed suffrage for African American women was crucial to protect their interests in an often discriminatory society. Burroughs defied societal restrictions placed on her gender and race, and she fought for greater rights for both African Americans and women.

Burroughs died in May 1961. In 1964, the school was renamed the Nannie Helen Burroughs School in her honor. Trades Hall, a National Historic Landmark, stands as a tangible reminder of Burroughs and her lifelong pursuit for racial and gender equality.

Associated Places:
Mary Church Terrell House, Washington, DC (designated a National Historic Landmark)

M Street High School, Washington, DC (listed on the National Register of Historic Places)

Trades Hall of the National Training School for Women and Girls (designated a National Historic Landmark)

—Katherine Crawford-Lackey

From Mannish Radicals to Feminist Heroes: Suffragists in Popular Culture

by Allison K. Lange

When you think of the women who advocated for the right to vote, which images come to mind? Perhaps you conjure up Susan B. Anthony's profile on the dollar coin or photographs of suffragists picketing the White House. Today, the popularity of these pictures reflects the growing interest in past female leaders. Their portraits cover the walls of museums, circulate on social media and in documentaries, and appear on protest posters. However, in the nineteenth century, many Americans mocked suffragists as ugly, masculine women. Elite white men were supposed to occupy visible positions of power. According to popular culture, political women rejected domestic life in favor of politics. Suffragists seemed to threaten the nation's values and traditions. Artists, editors, authors, publishers, and printers who held these views printed numerous cartoons that mocked the reformers. They reflected and defined the ways that Americans viewed female activists.

Suffragists quickly learned the power of these demeaning cartoons. Starting in the 1860s, they developed visual campaigns to counter them. To win support for their cause, they needed to transform popular visions of political women. First, they distributed portraits to establish an iconography of their leaders, especially for their supporters. By the turn of the century, they coordinated a national campaign to reach a much broader audience. Suffragists produced posters that represented

According to popular culture, political women rejected domestic life in favor of politics. Suffragists seemed to threaten the nation's values and traditions.

POPPING THE QUESTION
(A woman's right)

themselves as beautiful mothers, while newspaper photographs depicted them as fashionable picketers. These visual campaigns featured respectable white women and obscured suffragists of color. This signaled their choice not to fight for Black women's votes. The suffragists' visual campaigns changed the way Americans thought of political women. They continue to define our popular memory of the movement.[1]

* * *

The rise of women's rights activism in the 1840s was accompanied by a rise in mocking representations of female reformers in popular culture. Women's rights advocates sought better education and job opportunities, positions within the church, control over their own

Women's Rights. Engraving by David Claypoole Johnston, 1849.

money, and the vote.² Their demands sound reasonable today, but at the time they seemed dangerous to many Americans. This burst of activism coincided with the increasing circulation of illustrated weekly newspapers. Innovative new technology made engraved pictures cheap and accessible to more viewers than ever before.³ Lampooning female reformers became a popular amusement. Articles labeled these women ugly and sexless, while illustrations provided images of an unsettling future with these so-called monsters. Suffrage meetings and publications had a limited audience. Illustrated newspapers reached Americans across the country.

Cartoons warned that women would become like men physically and usurp men's separate spaces and roles if they gained political rights. In 1849, a year after the convention in Seneca Falls, New York, David Claypoole Johnston, a Boston-based engraver, circulated one such cartoon mocking female reformers in his publication *Scraps*.⁴ On the top right of the page, "Women's Tonsorial Rights" depicts a woman about to be shaved in a barbershop. To her right, a woman stands in an "unladylike" manner with her hands in her coat pockets and a cane. Another female customer with a cane reads the *Woman's Rights Advocate* as she sits with her feet up on a chair. On the left, a woman shaves herself using a mirror hanging on the wall. The scene recalls similar pictures of barbershops filled with men.⁵ Even the picture on the wall depicts female boxers. In this possible future, women would propose marriage—as in, "Popping the Question (A woman's right)"—and smoke in public—as in, "Women's Fumigatory Rights." Johnston's cartoons exemplify how artists, editors, and publishers employed pictures to police gender roles. They prompted laughter to undercut the cause.

Artists regularly drew cartoons similar to Johnston's, and reformers quickly recognized the damage they caused. As early as 1845, writer and thinker Margaret Fuller wrote about the popularity of such pictures in her book *Woman in the Nineteenth Century*. Opponents feared that if women became political, "The beauty of the home would be destroyed, the delicacy of the sex would be violated, the dignity of the halls of legislation degraded." Fuller argued that these anxieties resulted in the "ludicrous pictures of ladies in hysterics at the polls, and senate chambers filled with cradles." She countered that "woman can express publicly the fulness [*sic*] of thought and creation, without losing any of the particular beauty of her sex."⁶ Suffragists were not inherently hideous, masculine women who threatened "the beauty

Cartoons warned that women would become like men physically and usurp men's separate spaces and roles if they gained political rights.

of the home." However, since suffragists did not then publish popular newspapers, illustrated or not, they had little power to prove Fuller's point.

In the 1860s, suffragists began to distribute portraits of themselves to counter these cartoons. Sojourner Truth pioneered strategies for using photographs to challenge racist and sexist caricatures.[7] After escaping enslavement in New York in 1826, Truth became a women's rights and antislavery advocate. In 1850, she published her autobiography to raise money and awareness. A decade later, when new technology made reproducing photographs inexpensive, she decided to sell her portrait. By 1864, Truth had selected a preferred pose and props.[8] In one print, Truth, about age sixty-seven, sits next to a table with her knitting needles and work in her left hand. Her signature white head wrap, simple dark-colored dress, and modest shawl resemble Quaker attire.[9] The blank background draws the eye to her face, which has a serious expression. Her right hand grips the tail of her yarn, which snakes down her skirt as if the photographer interrupted her mid-stitch. Knitting alluded to feminine domesticity, but also represented a practical skill for any woman who sought to keep her family warm. The bouquet of flowers and table imply a parlor setting. Her book and wire-rimmed glasses reference her intelligence and inclusion in elite, educated circles. The pictures suggest that she subscribed to mainstream notions of femininity, even though her speeches declared no such thing.

Truth lacked the status of middle-class white women, so she used her photographic portrait to claim it. Her photographs telegraphed her modesty, intelligence, and Blackness. For Americans, who associated the visual medium with truthfulness, photographs provided evidence that other illustrations, with their visible marks of an artist's hand, did not. At that time, most white female reformers never sold their portraits. Keeping their likenesses private helped them maintain respectability in a society that frowned upon public, political women. In contrast, as stated on her picture, Truth sold her photograph— known at the time as a "shadow"—as a means to support herself, or the "substance." Unlike elite reformers, she needed the money for her livelihood. She copyrighted her picture, an unusual step at the time, to ensure that no one else profited. Truth sold it at her lectures, through reform papers, and her friends.[10] Some photographs were a larger cabinet size, but most were small, cheap *cartes de visite*. These photographs were roughly the size of a modern baseball card. By purchasing and displaying Truth's portrait, a buyer associated with her causes.

I Sell the Shadow to Support the Substance.
SOJOURNER TRUTH.

Sojourner Truth, ca. 1864. This was one of the *carte de visite* photographs that she copyrighted.

"The New Woman—Wash Day,"
stereograph image by R. Y. Young,
1901.

Taking a cue from Truth, the leaders of the new suffrage organization founded in 1869, the National Woman Suffrage Association, distributed portraits to construct their own public image of their movement. When Susan B. Anthony, Matilda Joslyn Gage, and Elizabeth Cady Stanton compiled the volumes of the *History of Woman Suffrage* in the 1870s, they spent significant money and time to print portraits of themselves and fellow white female leaders.[11] The series established an iconography of leaders who remain the most famous suffragists today. Anthony and Stanton portrayed suffragists in a similar manner to leading male politicians, encouraging viewers to imagine women as political leaders. The editors did not include portraits of Truth or any other Black reformers in their publications. They emphasized that refined white women sought the vote. Suffragists wanted to quell fears about increasing the number of Black voters. *The History of Woman Suffrage* marked a shift toward distributing portraits to define the movement's public image. The expense of the volumes, however, meant that their iconography still largely reached supporters rather than the general public.

Despite their efforts, popular publications still mocked suffragists. Technology changed, but pictures that ridiculed political women remained profitable.[12] Between 1871 and 1907, at least fifty different stereographs (and an unknown number of copies) lampooned the New Woman.[13] Stereographs were photographs that appeared three dimensional when viewed through a stereoscope. In one stereograph from 1901, a woman sits and reads a newspaper called the *Truth*, while her husband stands doing the laundry. The man stands over the washboard and glares at her. Labeled the "New Woman," the female figure reflects a new ideal of womanhood. The New Woman, according to this caricature, disdains female domesticity to seek an education, a profession, a social life, and a voice in politics. On the wall behind her is a picture of two women in their undergarments. The scene implies her rejection of heteronormative relationships as well. She disdains men and prefers for them to perform chores. Pictures like these recall visual themes established by cartoons such as Johnston's sixty years earlier. The suffragists produced innovative visual campaigns, but their opponents relied on familiar themes.

Over the course of the 1910s, support for woman suffrage gradually spread. Progressive Era reformers argued that female voters would help them achieve their goal of purifying politics. By 1915, eleven states had enfranchised women, and suffragists launched a major campaign to win the vote in New York, a center for publishing. In February 1915, *Puck*, a leading humor magazine that had regularly mocked the female reformers, printed an entire pro-suffrage issue. They did so under the editorial direction of a number of suffrage organizations. Readers could cut out the pictures and pin them to their walls. Suffrage organizations could have free copies of the illustrations. The editor had recognized that "The skilled 'campaigner' has learned the enormous value of a clever cartoon, a pithy editorial, used immediately and with telling effect." Hoping the new political stance would be profitable, the editor encouraged suffragists to "see that *Puck* comes into your home regularly." "Its propaganda value alone," he argued, "will balance the cost many times over."[14]

Our food, our health, our home, our schools,
our play are all regulated by men's votes——

Isn't it a funny thing
When father cannot see
Why mother ought to have a vote
On how these things should be?

"I'm a girl baby and I'm going to
be taxed without representation."

To be obtained as post cards from the
National Woman Suffrage Association,
Inc., 505 Fifth Ave., New York City.

Rose O'Neill, "Votes for Our Mothers," 1915.

As women gained access to education and a greater range of professions, female artists began designing suffrage imagery for widespread publication. *Puck* commissioned Rose O'Neill to draw pictures for its February 1915 issue. O'Neill, who regularly drew for *Puck*, represents a wave of professional female illustrators—such as Nina Allender, Blanche Ames, and Mary Ellen Sigsbee—who produced suffrage art for popular publications as well as suffrage papers.[15] Famous for her kewpies, one of O'Neill's pictures features four of the child-like figures marching in step. The leader holds a "Votes for Our Mothers" flag. With their large eyes and pleading looks, they appeal to parents who want to protect them. The accompanying stanza declares that men's votes regulate "our food, our health, our home, our schools, our play." The kewpies do not understand why "father cannot see / Why mother ought to have a vote / On how these things should be." A similar illustration on the right depicts a baby who is crying because she is "going to be taxed without representation." In both cases, the vulnerable kewpies emphasize their dependence on their parents—especially their mothers.

The most powerful suffrage group, the National American Woman Suffrage Association (NAWSA), published O'Neill's illustrations as part of its campaign to demonstrate that women needed the vote to protect their families. In the 1890s, NAWSA built up national and state press committees. By 1915, it had its own publishing company and employed publicity professionals to coordinate its public image. O'Neill's pictures articulated NAWSA's message perfectly. NAWSA distributed pictures to argue that white, motherly, political women would enhance—rather than threaten—traditional gender roles and American values. NAWSA had the most funding, expertise, and compelling message of any suffrage organization. During the 1910s, pictures with NAWSA's message dominated popular publications because they had the widest appeal.

NAWSA's imagery dominated, but other suffrage organizations orchestrated competing visual campaigns. The National Woman's Party (NWP) organized public protests, ranging from parades to pickets, and hired professional photographers to capture them.[16] The NWP incorporated tactics from British suffragists to win the public's attention.[17] Like NAWSA, it hired publicity professionals. The NWP wanted to promote a positive version of suffragists as pretty, educated, and white New Women. Newspapers across the country printed photographs of suffragists protesting in front of the White House. The pickets won the suffragists publicity as well as controversy. NAWSA leaders openly condemned NWP tactics. But the shocking photographs of picketers, followed by photographs of imprisoned suffragists accompanied by testimonies about terrible prison conditions, prompted public outcry. The negative response from the public forced officials to address the issue.

Organizations led by women of color contested the vision that more powerful suffrage groups promoted. But, they had less money and power to coordinate a visual campaign. NAWSA did not officially prevent Black women from joining, but local organizations could and did exclude them. As a result, Black women founded the National Association of Colored Women (NACW) in 1896 to fight for Black women's voting rights, improve education, and "uplift" Black communities. The NACW relied on the reform papers and individual leaders to promote a positive image of its cause.[18] Mary Church Terrell, the group's first president, became a model for the elegant, educated, and refined Black political womanhood the NACW promoted. Like Susan B. Anthony had done decades earlier, Terrell distributed portraits of

The most powerful suffrage group, the National American Woman Suffrage Association (NAWSA), published O'Neill's illustrations as part of its campaign to demonstrate that women needed the vote to protect their families.

herself. She also often worked with reform publications to promote the NACW's vision. Although its pictures reached fewer people, they countered the dominant image of suffragists to create opportunities for women of color.

Over the course of their movement, suffragists gradually developed visual campaigns to challenge the popular, disparaging cartoons of political women. Their propaganda presented an appealing image of female voters to win support for the cause. The campaigns carried out by the comparatively well-funded NAWSA and NWP advocated for the rights of white women, especially those of the middle and upper classes. They promoted heteronormative families and white supremacy to quell concerns that female voters would threaten these longstanding American values. These suffragists did not include women of color in their vision or feature leaders such as Sojourner Truth and Mary Church Terrell as faces of the cause. White suffragists followed through on the promises of their visual campaign. They chose not to ensure that all women could vote after the amendment's passage. Black, Puerto Rican, Native American, and Asian women continued to fight for voting rights long after 1920.

The imagery promoted by suffragists and their opponents still resonates today. Cartoons of suffragists might seem distant, but the image of the masculine, angry feminist who threatens American values still appears in the media. The suffragists' visual campaign to transform popular ideas about gender and politics still defines the way we remember the movement in museums and documentaries. Their pictures incorporated what are now outdated ideas about gender, race, class, and sexuality. Yet their vision remains relevant. Female politicians still position themselves as mothers who entered politics to improve life for their families. Protestors capture the attention of the press, but women who adhere to a more traditional vision of womanhood tend to occupy visible government positions. A more modern vision of gender and politics, however, rather than rewarding elite white women who perform a complicated balancing act of femininity and political power, could require less engagement with outdated social norms. New images and ideas could provide new opportunities for women in twenty-first-century politics.

The imagery promoted by suffragists and their opponents still resonates today. Cartoons of suffragists might seem distant, but the image of the masculine, angry feminist who threatens American values still appears in the media.

Wilhelmina Kekelaokalaninui Widemann Dowsett

Wilhelmina Kekelaokalaninui Widemann Dowsett was born in Lihue, Kauai in the Kingdom of Hawai'i in 1861. Her mother, Mary Kaumana Pilahiuilani, was a Native Hawaiian, and her father was a German immigrant.

In 1893, pro-American interests, with the assistance of US Marines, overthrew Queen Lili'uokalani and established the Republic of Hawai'i. The former island nation was annexed to the United States in 1898. When this happened, women in Hawai'i sought voting rights just like mainland suffragists.

In 1912, Dowsett founded the National Women's Equal Suffrage Association of Hawai'i (WESAH). It was the first Hawaiian suffrage organization. Modeling its constitution on that of the National American Woman Suffrage Association (NAWSA), they invited mainland suffragists to speak to the group. One of these women included Carrie Chapman Catt.

Thanks to the efforts of women like Dowsett and WESAH, President Wilson signed a bill allowing the residents of the territory to decide for themselves. Both Native Hawaiian and white suffragists gathered at the capitol building (formerly known as 'Iolani Palace) on the morning of the Senate vote on March 4, 1919. Many in the

territory, like those on the mainland, were against granting the right of suffrage to Asian women. Dowsett, however, included them in her vision of Hawai'i's future. The bill passed the Hawaiian Senate that day, but a fresh battle was waiting in the House. Instead of granting women's suffrage immediately, the House decided to put it to a vote of the Hawaiian electorate in 1920. Furious with that response, Dowsett and 500 other women of "various nationalities, of all ages" poured onto the House floor with banners demanding "Votes for Women." Forced to reckon with the demonstrators, the House held hearings the next day for proponents and opponents to make their case.

A month later, the House had not budged and the suffragists of Hawai'i were losing their patience. Regrouping, Dowsett and her group began to lobby directly to the US Congress through the territorial representative, Prince Kūhiō. They also began to create grassroots groups throughout the territory to prepare women for the vote when that opportunity arrived.

Hawaiian women became enfranchised along with their mainland sisters when the Nineteenth Amendment became part of the US Constitution in August 1920. As residents of a US territory, however, their elected representation was limited. It would take another 39 years for Hawai'i to become the 50th state in the Union, and for the residents of Hawai'i, both male and female, to gain full US voting rights. Dowsett did not live long enough to see that day; she died December 10, 1929. She is buried in Oahu Cemetery, Honolulu.

> **Associated Places:**
> Cathedral Church of Saint Andrew, Honolulu, Hawai'i (listed on the National Register of Historic Places)
>
> 'Iolani Palace, Honolulu, Hawai'i (listed on the National Register of Historic Places and designated a National Historic Landmark)
>
> —Katherine Crawford-Lackey

Woman Suffrage in the West

by Jennifer Helton

Decades before passage of the Nineteenth Amendment, western women voted and served in public office. In the diverse West, woman suffragists campaigned across mountains, plains, and deserts. They found common cause with a variety of communities and other political movements.

Women of the West were the first in the United States to enjoy full voting rights. As new territories and states organized, many considered, and most granted, women the right to vote. Decades before passage of the Nineteenth Amendment, western women voted and served in public office. In the diverse West, woman suffragists campaigned across mountains, plains, and deserts. They found common cause with a variety of communities and other political movements. Though they experienced setbacks along with their early victories, their successes were crucial to the eventual passage of a federal suffrage amendment.

The first attempt to secure woman suffrage in the West took place in 1854, when the territorial legislature of Washington considered a suffrage measure. It was defeated by a single vote.[1] However, it wasn't until the Reconstruction era, after the end of the Civil War that the suffrage movement in the West truly began. The abolition of slavery in 1865 prompted a national deliberation about citizenship and voting rights. During the debates on the Fourteenth and Fifteenth Amendments, women's rights advocates lobbied—unsuccessfully—to enshrine woman suffrage in the Constitution. As attention then turned to the states, many supporters saw the West, with its young governments, as fertile territory for experiments with political reforms.

In February 1868, suffragist Laura De Force Gordon created a sensation by lecturing about woman suffrage in San Francisco. She followed up by giving several suffrage talks in Nevada before returning to California to organize suffrage societies. Perhaps inspired by Gordon, the 1869 Nevada legislature passed an amendment to eliminate the words "male" and "white" from the voting requirements in the state constitution. Nevada law required that constitutional changes be passed in two sessions of the legislature. Suffrage advocates would have to wait until 1871 to see if the amendment would be confirmed.[2]

So, it was the women of Wyoming Territory, on December 10, 1869, who were the first to gain the vote. Several suffragist women in the territory, including Esther Morris and Amalia Post, likely lobbied behind the scenes for the law. But Reconstruction politics also played a role. Governor John Allen Campbell, Territorial Secretary Edward Lee, and other federally appointed Republican officials supported universal equal rights.

But it was Democrat William Bright who introduced the voting rights bill in the legislature. A southerner, Bright—whose wife, Julia, supported woman suffrage—opposed voting rights for African Americans. He had vehemently spoken out against the Fourteenth Amendment, fearing it would enfranchise Black men. If Black men were to be given the vote, Bright believed, women—and particularly white women—should be as well. Once enfranchised, Wyoming women enthusiastically exercised their new rights. They voted, ran for office, and eventually served in elected positions. Esther Morris became the first woman in the United States to serve as a judge, and Amalia Post was one of the first to serve on a jury.[3]

Utah's predominantly Mormon territorial legislature enfranchised its women soon after, on February 12, 1870. Though Mormon women generally did not espouse radical views about female equality, they had long held the right to vote within church assemblies.[4] In late 1869, Congress attempted to eliminate polygamy in Utah Territory by proposing the Collum Act. This Act would deny suffrage to men who supported plural

On this scrapbook page, NAWSA president Carrie Chapman Catt commemorated Wyoming Territory's passage of the first full woman suffrage law in the nation. William Bright was the legislator who proposed the bill, and women's rights advocate Esther Morris became the first female justice of the peace.

THIS TABLET MARKS THE SITE WHERE THE COUNCIL OF THE FIRST TERRITORIAL LEGISLATURE OF WYOMING CONVENED WHICH LEGISLATURE ENACTED THE FIRST WOMAN SUFFRAGE LAW PASSED IN THE UNITED STATES

APPROVED BY JOHN ALLEN CAMPBELL FIRST GOVERNOR OF WYOMING DECEMBER 10, 1869

PLACED BY CHEYENNE CHAPTER DAUGHTERS OF THE AMERICAN REVOLUTION 1917

Mrs. Esther Morris. The woman who led Wyoming to grant the vote to women.

William H. Bright. who introduced the bill to give votes to women in Wyoming's first Legislature, 1869.

BUILDING AT CHEYENNE, WYOMING, WHERE THE FIRST TERRITORIAL COUN-CIL OF THE LEGISLATURE MET, AND WHERE WAS INTRODUCED THE BILL WHICH GAVE WOMEN THE RIGHT OF SUFFRAGE
From a sketch made by Governor Carey

marriage. On January 13, 1870, three thousand Utah women gathered in the Salt Lake Tabernacle at a "Great Indignation Meeting" to protest the law. Fourteen women rose to speak in defense of polygamy and women's rights, including several who called for the right to vote.[5] After the legislature passed the woman suffrage bill, Utah women immediately began to exercise their rights. They voted in a Salt Lake City municipal election only two days after the bill passed.[6] Eliza Snow, who had been the wife of both Joseph Smith and Brigham Young, deemed it "as necessary to vote as to pray."[7]

These early successes can be attributed partly to lack of organized opposition. In Wyoming, woman suffrage was supported by politicians from both parties, though for different reasons. In Utah, suffragists were supported by the Mormon Church. After these victories, many hoped that the 1871 Nevada legislature would reaffirm the suffrage act it had passed in 1869. But despite lobbying efforts by Laura De Force Gordon and Emily Pitts Stevens, also of California, the measure failed.[8] Nevada's women would wait until 1914 to vote. In the other states and territories of the West, too, suffragists would encounter active resistance.

By 1870, women who hoped to spread suffrage through the West began to organize. In some areas, suffragists formed chapters of the national suffrage organizations. In others, they worked through women's clubs. Black clubwomen were particularly committed to the cause. They organized suffrage societies in Idaho, Montana, North Dakota, Nevada, Arizona, Oklahoma, and New Mexico.[9] The Woman's Christian Temperance Union (WCTU), which had chapters across the West, also supported suffrage. The temperance movement inspired many women to agitate for the vote. But it also motivated well-funded opponents, in particular, the "liquor interests."

In the 1870s and 1880s, women's organizations fought many campaigns, but they had limited success. In 1870, the governor of Colorado Territory, Edward McCook, announced his support for woman suffrage. After heated debate, however, the legislature rejected a suffrage measure.[10] When Colorado became a state in 1876, activists' efforts to include suffrage in the state constitution failed. So, too, did a subsequent 1877 referendum.[11] Two more unsuccessful legislative attempts followed in 1881 and 1891.[12] Opposition of the liquor interests contributed to these defeats. Anti-Chinese racism was also a factor. One anti-suffrage argument warned: "the poor, degraded Chinese women who might reach our shores, would also be admitted to the voting list, and what then would become of our proud, Caucasian civilization?"[13] Better not to enfranchise any women at all.

In California, too, suffragists regularly lobbied the legislature to approve women's voting rights, but it steadfastly refused.[14] As in Colorado, anti-Chinese racism was strong, even among suffragists. At the 1879 California constitutional convention, suffrage leaders embraced the anti-Chinese rhetoric of the Workingmen's Party, hoping to gain its support. In the end, woman suffrage was not included in the new constitution, though anti-Chinese provisions were.[15]

Further north, in the Pacific Northwest, Oregon activist Abigail Scott Duniway and national suffrage leader Susan B. Anthony embarked upon a two thousand-mile journey across Oregon and Washington in 1871. They delivered lectures and organized suffrage clubs as they went.[16] Duniway and other suffragists succeeded in getting bills introduced in the Oregon legislature in 1871, 1873, 1875, and 1884. Despite this, the only success for Oregon women in this era was passage in 1877 of a school suffrage law.[17]

For a time, the situation in Washington Territory looked brighter. Activist Mary Olney Brown attempted to vote in 1869, and in 1870 a few women successfully voted. They argued that as citizens it was their right under the Fourteenth Amendment. This prompted the legislature to pass a bill forbidding voting for women. Attempts to pass suffrage bills in 1878 and 1881 failed.[18]

Nonetheless, suffragists pressed on. In 1883 the Washington territorial legislature passed woman suffrage. For four years, women voted. Then, in 1887, Washington's Supreme Court invalidated the suffrage law on a technicality. When the legislature responded by passing a new suffrage law, opponents, supported by the anti-temperance machine, fired back with a lawsuit. The Supreme Court again declared woman suffrage invalid, on the shakiest of grounds. In 1890, like Oregon women, Washington women were granted school suffrage in place of full voting rights.[19]

Washington women were not alone in losing voting rights. Congress deprived Utah women of the right to vote with the Edmunds-Tucker Act of 1887. This law disenfranchised all Utah women, as well as men who practiced polygamy. Utah suffragist Charlotte Godbe and Belva Lockwood, one of the first female lawyers in the United States, tried unsuccessfully to lobby against this bill. When it passed, in the words of Utah suffragist Emmeline Wells, it "wrested from all the women, Gentile and Mormon alike, the suffrage which they had exercised for seventeen years."[20] In response, women founded the Woman Suffrage Association of Utah.

Further north, in the Pacific Northwest, Oregon activist Abigail Scott Duniway and national suffrage leader Susan B. Anthony embarked upon a two thousand-mile journey across Oregon and Washington in 1871. They delivered lectures and organized suffrage clubs as they went.

A SAMPLING OF WESTERN SUFFRAGE NEWSPAPERS

Newspaper	Editor(s)	Location	Year Established
Pioneer	Emily Pitts Stevens	San Francisco	1865
New Northwest	Abigail Scott Duniway	Oregon	1871
Women's Exponent	Louisa Green Richards, Emmeline B. Wells	Utah	1872
Queen Bee	Caroline Nichols Church	Colorado	1879
Woman's Tribune	Clara Bewick Colby	Nebraska, later Oregon	1883

Facing page: Women's newspapers, like the *Woman's Exponent*, played a critical role in building a community of pro-suffrage women in the West. Founded and primarily authored by women, these papers articulated the arguments for suffrage and refuted arguments against it. They also shared news of female activism from across the US and around the world.

Despite these frustrations and defeats, in the 1870s and 1880s western activists laid the groundwork for later successes. An important step was their establishment of regional suffrage newspapers. Woman suffrage papers laid out the arguments for suffrage and helped to create a community of activists. They connected western women to the suffrage work that was happening around the world. Western women also wrote for national papers, keeping the women back East informed about progress in the West. In Colorado, for example, Elizabeth Ensley was a correspondent for the *Woman's Era*, a nationwide African American women's paper.[21] Though the achievements of the 1870s and 1880s were limited, the struggles of this period gave activists the experience, networks, and knowledge they would need for later efforts.

By the 1890s, these factors, combined with new political alliances, contributed to new gains. Wyoming entered the Union as a state in 1890 with woman suffrage intact. It was the first state, as it had been the first territory, to guarantee its women the right to vote. The federal government became receptive to Utah's application for statehood once the Mormon Church outlawed polygamy in 1890. At the Utah constitutional convention in 1895, Utah's suffragists lobbied to ensure that women were included. When Utah became a state in 1896, Utah women regained the right to vote.[22]

It was not until 1893, however, that the West saw its first successful statewide referendum campaign, in Colorado. There, local and national suffrage societies partnered with new labor and political organizations to

Woman's Exponent.

VOL. I.   SALT LAKE CITY, UTAH, JUNE 1, 1872.   No. 1.

NEWS AND VIEWS.

Women are now admitted to fifty American colleges.

Rev. De Witt Talmage is pronounced a success as a sensation preacher.

Theodore Tilton says the best brains in northern New York are wearing white hats. They might wear chapeaux of a more objectionable color.

Daniel W. Voorhees in one day destroyed the political record of a life-time, and that was when he became henchman to a judge with an ecclesiastical mission.

An Alabama editor writes "United State," and refuses to write "United States"—a straw to show how Southern sentiment runs. What a state he must be in?

The season of scattering intellectual filth has set in over the country. It occurs quadrennially in the United States, commencing a few months before the Presidential election.

Dr. Newman failed to become a Bishop at the Methodist General Conference, and Dr. Newman mourns this second great defeat. He has remembrances of Salt Lake in connection with the previous one.

Great outcry is raised against the much marrying of the Latter-day Saints. The tendency of the age is to disregard marriage altogether, but there seems no indication of a desire to have the race die out.

The "Alabama" muddle like "confusion worse confounded" becomes worse mixed the more it is stirred. It stretches itself over the path of time, and "like a wounded snake drags its slow length along." The country has become heartily sick of it.

Some Eastern journals head their Utah news with "Deseret." With keen appreciation of the coming and inevitable, they accept the mellifluous name chosen for the region wrested by that industry which "the honey bee" represents, from the barren wilds of nature.

George Francis Train sends us a bundle of Train Ligues. The compliment is appreciated, but the act is like sweetness wasted. We can vote, but not for "the next President of America." Utah has not become Deseret yet, nor can it participate in President making.

The last week of May, 1872, will be memorable in American annals as the first time since the first ordinance of secession was passed in the South, that both houses of Congress had their full list of members. Statesmanship can retain a complete Federal legislature, but the article has grown somewhat scarce.

To pardon the worst class of criminals on condition that they emigrate to the United States, is growing in favor with European monarchies. Germany and Greece so far have done the largest business in this line, the latest batch of villains thus disposed of being the Marathon murderers from Greece. Orders have been forwarded by President Grant to New Orleans, to which port it is understood they have been sent, to prevent their landing. They should be captured, ironed, returned to Athens with Uncle Samuel's compliments, and a bill for direct and "consequential" damages presented.

News comes from France that trailing dresses for street wear are going out of fashion. So many absurd and ridiculous fashions come from Paris that the wonder is thinking American women do not, with honest republican spirit, reject them entirely. This latter one, however, is so sensible that its immediate adoption will be an evidence of good sense wisely directed.

The anti-Mormon bill of Judge Bingham seems to have fared no better in the judiciary committee of the House of Representatives than the one to which Mr. Voorhees stood sponsor. It is gratifying to think that a majority of that committee yet respect the antiquated and once revered instrument still occasionally referred to as the Constitution.

Rev. James Freeman Clark claims "that if it is an advantage to vote, women ought to have it; if a disadvantage men ought not to be obliged to bear it alone." Speaking from experience we feel safe in affirming that the Rev. gentleman is right, and we hope for a time when this immunity may be universally enjoyed by our pure-minded and light-loving sisters. We don't presume that those belonging to the opposite class care anything about it.

Mrs. Carrie F. Young, editor of the "Pacific Journal of Health," has been lecturing in Idaho on Temperance and Woman Suffrage. The editor of the "Idaho World" was not present, but did not regret his absence. He says, "We feel a most decided repugnance to the exhibition of a woman upon the rostrum, advocating such degrading theories as 'woman suffrage' and other cognate subjects." He omits to state whether "Temperance" is one of the "degrading theories" to which he refers.

Force is ever the argument of a bad cause. The principles which cannot be overcome except by the exercise of physical power, present a front that arrests the attention of thinking minds. Where argument fails and force is employed to overcome an opponent, the power of the principles to which opposition is made is admitted. Will those who urge repressive legislation against the people of Utah think of it? Witness the Voorhees bill as an illustration.

A notable event, as a result of the late terrible Franco-German war, is the opening of the German University in Strasbourg, which takes place June 1st—to-day. That famous city on the Rhine, after a siege memorable in the annals of warfare, passed into the hands of the Germans, and now they take the surest means to permanently consolidate their power, by establishing there one of those seats of learning for which Germany has become enviably famous.

Miss Susan B. Anthony, it is said, declared before the Cincinnati Convention met, that if it gave her cause "the cold shoulder," she would go to Philadelphia and pledge the ballots of the women of America to U. S. Grant. As the women of America are yet without ballots, and as it is very questionable, if they had them, whether they would authorize any single individual to pledge them for any candidate, the supposition is fair that Miss Anthony possesses too much good sense to have made any such declaration.

Rev. Mr. Peirce, a Methodist clergyman who has made Salt Lake his headquarters for some time, in lecturing east proposed the extinction of polygamy by the introduction here of vast quantities of expensive millinery goods, and by inducing "Gentile" women to dress in gorgeous style that "Mormon" women might imitate them and run up such heavy dry goods bills that it would be impossible for a man to support more than one wife, if even one. Mr. Peirce, no doubt, preaches modesty and humility occasionally, by way of variety; now he recommends the encouragement of pride, vanity and extravagance to accomplish his "Christian" designs. The course he advises has been largely followed in many places, has tenanted brothels, aided to fill prisons, broken up families, hurled women of reputation and position down to degradation and infamy, and has met heavy denunciations from inspired men whom Mr. Peirce professes to revere. He would steal the livery of evil to serve religion in. There is not much of this reverend gentleman, and that little there is must be either very silly or very wicked.

The editor of "The Present Age" has been to a church and heard an orthodox sermon, in which the preacher took occasion to say that all religious "isms," including Mohammedanism, Mormonism and Spiritualism, rested their claims for being true "upon miracles." The "Age" is a Spiritualist and denies that his "ism" basis its claims to be true upon miracles. Latter-day Saints deny that Mormonism basis any claim for credence in it on miracles; the reverse is the truth. The "Age" defines a miracle to be "the setting aside for the time being of a natural law to meet an unexpected emergency." Had he said a miracle was the bringing into operation of certain natural laws not generally understood or comprehended, he would have been nearer correct. When somebody can tell how a natural law may be or can be set aside, except by the operation of some other natural law, his definition, which is the generally received one, may be entitled to more consideration. We imagine the working of the overland telegraph is as great a miracle to the Cheyenne Indians as any recorded miracle that the "Age" or the orthodox minister can quote.

Mrs. Laura De Force Gordon attended the Cincinnati Convention and claimed a seat as a delegate from California. Her claim was treated with hisses and laughter. She took a position in front of the stand and endeavored to speak, but her voice was drowned by a tumultuous discord. Her persistence in seeking to address an assemblage that treated her claim in such a manner was undignified; while the action of the Convention in receiving her with hisses and uproarious laughter, was disgraceful. The Liberal Republicans assembled in Cincinnati for a general work of purification and reform, evidently stood greatly in need of general reform themselves, in the matter of manners as well as in politics. Mrs. Gordon was as much entitled to a seat in that Convention as Carl Schurz himself, for we have yet to learn that the call for it specified that "male" Republicans only were admissable.

A new periodical in London is called "The Ladies."

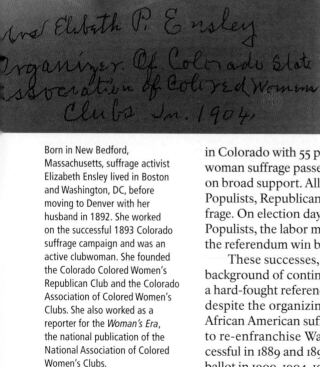

Mrs Elizbeth P. Ensley Organizer. Of Colorado State Association of Colored Womens Clubs Jn. 1904,

Born in New Bedford, Massachusetts, suffrage activist Elizabeth Ensley lived in Boston and Washington, DC, before moving to Denver with her husband in 1892. She worked on the successful 1893 Colorado suffrage campaign and was an active clubwoman. She founded the Colorado Colored Women's Republican Club and the Colorado Association of Colored Women's Clubs. She also worked as a reporter for the *Woman's Era*, the national publication of the National Association of Colored Women's Clubs.

win support. In the early 1890s, six Denver women, including African American activist Elizabeth P. Ensley, founded the Colorado Equal Suffrage Association. It was later known as the Non-Partisan Equal Suffrage Association. Ensley, who served as treasurer of the association during the 1893 campaign, ensured that African American activists were connected to the movement. Suffragists also made common cause with the Knights of Labor and the Populist Party. These organizations had women leaders and members and were influential in farming and mining communities. The support of national suffrage leaders also contributed to the Colorado victory. Carrie Chapman Catt, who arrived in Colorado to organize on behalf of the National American Woman Suffrage Association (NAWSA), traveled over one thousand miles across the state, lecturing and founding suffrage clubs. Coalition politics proved successful; woman suffrage passed in Colorado with 55 percent of the vote. In Idaho, too, woman suffrage passed by referendum and depended on broad support. All three major parties in Idaho—Populists, Republicans, and Democrats—endorsed suffrage. On election day in November 1896, support from Populists, the labor movement, and Mormons helped the referendum win by a two-to-one margin.[23]

These successes, however, took place against a background of continued setbacks elsewhere. In 1896, a hard-fought referendum campaign in California failed, despite the organizing efforts of Anthony, Catt, and African American suffragist Naomi Anderson. Attempts to re-enfranchise Washington's women were unsuccessful in 1889 and 1898. In Oregon, suffrage was on the ballot in 1900, 1904, 1906, 1908, and 1910 and lost each time.[24] In other states, women continued to organize. The Montana Woman Suffrage Association, established in the 1890s, grew rapidly under the leadership of Populist Ella Knowles. She was also Montana's assistant attorney general. Arizona women founded the Arizona Woman's Equal Rights Association in 1887. In Nevada, educator Eliza Clapp and others formed the Nevada Equal Suffrage Association (NESA) in 1895. In all these states, suffrage organizations lobbied their legislatures nearly every session, with few results.[25]

Finally, after a fourteen-year gap, a wave of enfranchisements took place in the 1910s. The western suffrage campaigns of this era often rejected the involvement of NAWSA, whose methods had been unsuccessful in the 1890s and early 1900s. Instead, the new generation formed partnerships with the Progressive and socialist movements. Having learned the hard lessons of earlier failures, they also disassociated themselves from temperance.[26]

The breakthrough came in 1910, when Washington became the fifth state to grant full suffrage. Led by Emma Smith DeVoe and May Arkwright Hutton, a new generation of suffragists took up the fight.[27] Dr. Cora Smith Eaton led a group of suffragists up Mount Rainier, where they staked a green pennant proclaiming "VOTES FOR WOMEN" at the peak.[28] Campaigners rented billboards, participated in parades, and even sponsored a whistle-stop train tour. Strong links with the labor movement, which was fighting for an eight-hour-day bill for women, were also critical. The campaigners were quick to connect woman suffrage to popular Progressive causes and steered clear of temperance. Finally, fifty-six years after the first attempt to enfranchise Washington women, the measure passed with nearly 64 percent of the vote.[29]

In California, Progressive legislators placed a woman suffrage measure on the 1911 ballot. The massive campaign that followed favored bold approaches. These included building suffrage parade floats, presenting stereopticon shows to amazed audiences, and plastering suffrage posters on every available surface. Clubwomen, Progressives,

This California Equal Suffrage Association flyer illustrates the pro-suffrage arguments used by activists in the early 1900s—traditional American rhetoric around equality before the law, no taxation without representation, and the dignity of labor—that allowed suffragists to build broad coalitions of supporters.

WOMAN SUFFRAGE IN THE WESTERN STATES

Territory / State	Year Women Fully Enfranchised and Method by Which Suffrage Was Achieved
Wyoming Territory and State	1869: Act of Territorial Legislature 1890: Included in State Constitution
Utah Territory and State	1870: Woman suffrage passed by Utah Territorial Legislature 1887: Suffrage revoked by Congress 1896: Suffrage restored by Utah State Constitution
State of Colorado	1893 via Referendum
State of Idaho	1896 via Referendum
Washington Territory and State	1883: Woman suffrage passed by Washington Territorial Legislature 1887: Suffrage struck down by Washington Supreme Court 1910: Suffrage restored via referendum
State of California	1911 via Referendum
State of Arizona	1912 via Initiative
Alaska Territory	1912 via Act of Legislature
State of Oregon	1912 via Initiative
State of Montana	1914 via Referendum
State of Nevada	1914 via Referendum
State of New Mexico	1920 via Passage of the Nineteenth Amendment
Territory of Hawai'i	1920 via Passage of the Nineteenth Amendment

and Socialists all worked for the cause, and the College Equal Suffrage League and the Wage Earners Suffrage League played important roles. California's diverse communities provided essential support. Suffrage articles appeared in Spanish, Chinese, German, Portuguese, and Italian. Maria de Lopez, a Los Angeles clubwoman, campaigned and translated at rallies in Southern California, where suffragists distributed tens of thousands of pamphlets in Spanish. In Oakland, members of the Colored Women's Suffrage League monitored polling stations to prevent fraud. And though hostility to Chinese Americans lingered among some white activists, others courted their support. A majority of Chinese voters supported suffrage on election day. Woman suffrage passed with a mere 50.7 percent of the vote.[30] Once again, coalitions had worked.

Oregon finally enfranchised its women via referendum in 1912, after campaigners embraced parades, publicity, and coalitions. At least twenty-three suffrage clubs existed in Portland alone. Jewish women held key leadership roles on the Portland Central Campaign Committee. The Colored Women's Equal Suffrage Association organized Black churchwomen. The Chinese American Suffrage Club mobilized Portland's Chinese neighborhoods. Politicians and labor leaders dominated the Men's Equal Suffrage Club. Portland suffragists also had a boys' club, a Quaker club, and a stenographers' club. Unions, farmers, Socialists, and the WCTU all endorsed voting rights for women. In the end, the measure squeaked through with 52 percent of the vote.[31] As in California, diverse coalitions were essential to overcome the opposition of liquor interests and old guard machine politics.

Women in Arizona and the new territory of Alaska

This pamphlet, published by the Los Angeles Political Equality League, makes the case for woman suffrage in Spanish. In the successful 1911 campaign, suffrage organizations, which were often led by and centered on the concerns of Anglo women, made efforts to gain the support of the Latinx community. Some Latina leaders saw the vote as a means to protect their communities.

Dese a la Mujer de California El Derecho de Votar

VOTOS PARA LA MUJER

POR QUE

PORQUE, la mujer debe obedecer la ley como el hombre,
Debe votar como el hombre.

PORQUE, la mujer paga contribuciones como el hombre, sosteniendo asi el gobierno,
Debe votar como el hombre.

PORQUE, la mujer sufre por mal gobierno como el hombre,
Debe votar como el hombre.

PORQUE, las madres quieren mejorar las condiciones de sus hijos,
Debe votar como el hombre.

PORQUE, mas de 6,000,000 de mujeres en los Estados Unidos trabajan, y su salud asi como la de nuestros futuros ciudadanos esta con frecuencia en peligro con motivo de las malas condiciones de los talleres, que solo pueden ser remediadas por medio de la legislatura,
Debe votar como el hombre.

PORQUE, la mujer acomodada que trata de ayudar al bienestar del publico, podria sostener su opinión por medio de su voto,
Debe votar como el hombre.

PORQUE, la hacendosa ama de casa y la mujer de profesion no pueden dar ese servicio al público y solo pueden servir al Estado por el mismo método usado por los hombres de negocios, es decir, por medio del voto,
Debe votar como el hombre.

PORQUE, la mujer necesita ser educada á mayor altura acerca de su responsibilidad en el sentido social y civico y ésto solo se desarrolla con el uso.
Debe votar como el hombre.

PORQUE, la mujer es consumidora y los consumidores necesitan absoluta representacion en politica,
Debe votar como el hombre.

PORQUE, las mujeres ciudadanas de un gobierno formado del pueblo, elejido POR el pueblo y PARA el pueblo.
Debe votar como el hombre.

LA MUJER lo necesita.
EL HOMBRE lo necesita.
EL ESTADO lo necesita.

PORQUE

¿POR QUE?

La mujer debe dar su ayuda.
El Hombre debe dar su ayuda.
El Estado debe usar su ayuda.

also won the right to vote in 1912. When Arizona became a state in 1912, its constitution did not guarantee woman suffrage. After an attempt to secure a referendum failed, the Arizona Equal Suffrage Association (AESA) gathered enough signatures on petitions to place an initiative on the ballot. The AESA secured the support of both the Republican and Democratic Parties. They also reached out to Progressives, socialists, and the labor movement. Some suffragists used racist and nativist arguments, claiming that native-born American white women deserved the right to vote more than foreign-born immigrant men. At the same time, however, the AESA worked with Mexican American organizations, Spanish newspapers, and immigrant miners. The measure passed by a two-to-one margin. Support from Mormons and Progressives was key to its success.[32] In Alaska, things were a bit easier. NAWSA sent literature to legislators of the new territory, who quickly proposed a bill. Woman suffrage was the first law signed by the governor.[33]

Two years later, Montana granted women the vote. Jeannette Rankin, a Montanan and NAWSA organizer who had worked on suffrage efforts across the country, led the campaign. She sent speakers into nearly every mining community in the state. One of her organizers, Maggie Smith Hardaway, delivered fifty-five talks and traveled 2,375 miles over seven weeks. At the state fair in September, the Montana State Men's League for Woman Suffrage marched in a suffrage parade. The WCTU was not allowed to make an appearance at the event for fear of rousing the saloon lobby. The referendum squeaked by, with 52.2 percent of voters approving it.[34]

The Nevada legislature finally passed successive woman suffrage referenda in 1911 and 1913. They then sent the measure to the voters for a final decision. Anne Martin of the Nevada Equal Suffrage Association (NESA) led the Nevada campaign. Martin had been involved with the radical suffrage movement in Britain. She led the NESA in establishing new clubs, publicizing the cause in the press, and distributing suffrage literature across the state. Margaret Foley, a labor organizer from Boston, "talked in the depths of eight mines, attended fifty dances, made one thousand speeches, and [wore] out three pairs of shoes." The Socialist, Democratic, and Progressive Parties endorsed woman suffrage at their conventions. These efforts paid off. The referendum passed by a wide margin, finally ending the struggle that had begun in 1869.[35]

With Nevada's vote, only New Mexico, of the continental western states, did not grant women full voting rights before the Nineteenth Amendment. Attempts to gain woman suffrage failed in 1871 and 1891, and the state constitution of 1910 granted only school suffrage. Hispano delegates to the 1910 constitutional convention secured stringent protections for Spanish American (male) voting rights. To protect themselves against any future attempts at Jim Crow-style disenfranchisement, Hispano delegates demanded measures that made voting provisions practically unamendable.[36] These measures also made it impossible to enfranchise New Mexico's women by referendum. A different strategy was needed.

The Congressional Union (CU), founded by radical suffragist Alice Paul, began organizing in New Mexico in the early 1910s. In 1917, the CU, by then renamed the National Woman's Party (NWP), recruited Adelina Otero-Warren, a member of a prominent Republican Hispano family, to oversee its work in New Mexico. Otero-Warren led the NWP's New Mexico campaign for ratification of the Nineteenth Amendment. Suffrage pamphlets were printed in Spanish, and Otero-Warren, along with Aurora Lucero and other local suffragists, promoted the cause.[37] New Mexico ratified the Nineteenth Amendment in February 1920.

Not all western women, however, received the vote with ratification of the Nineteenth Amendment. Many Native American women were not considered US citizens and thus were not able to vote. Nor did state suffrage laws enfranchise indigenous women, unless they had renounced their connection to their tribe. Suffragists only infrequently reached out to native communities. Some indigenous leaders, however, believed that voting rights could be a powerful tool for protecting native rights. In 1924 Zitkala-Sa, a Lakota writer and activist, lobbied Congress to secure suffrage for indigenous Americans. Partly as a result of her efforts, Congress passed the Indian Citizenship Act, which defined Native Americans as US citizens.

A descendant of two of the oldest Spanish families in New Mexico, Adelina "Nina" Otero-Warren led the New Mexico chapter of Alice Paul's Congressional Union, organizing and lecturing in both Spanish and English. She also served as superintendent of schools for Santa Fe County from 1917 to 1929 and ran unsuccessfully for the US House of Representatives in 1922.

Even after passage of this law, however, many western states continued to disenfranchise indigenous people. Zitkala-Sa went on to cofound the National Council of American Indians, which focused on civil rights for native peoples.[38]

The Territory of Hawai'i also exemplified the challenges faced by indigenous women. After the last indigenous ruler of Hawai'i, Queen Lili'uokalani, was deposed by the United States in 1893, local WCTU activists lobbied for the inclusion of women in the territorial government. When the Territory of Hawai'i was created in 1898, however, woman suffrage was specifically excluded. This was partly because indigenous women significantly outnumbered white women in the territory.[39]

For women who were able to vote, enfranchisement paved the way for their entry into politics. Across the West, women won election to office, most often for school boards or as county superintendent of schools. In the 1890s, Colorado, Idaho, and Utah all elected women to their state legislatures.[40] The West produced the first woman governor, Nellie Tayloe Ross of Wyoming. She later served as director of the US Mint. The West also elected Jeannette Rankin of Montana the first woman to sit in Congress.

The enfranchisement of women in the United States began in the West. Early successes there were connected to the complex politics of Reconstruction and polygamy. Later victories stemmed from suffragists' ability to build partnerships with other movements that shared their desire for reform and increased democratization of politics. Over time, suffragists discovered that campaigns were most likely to succeed when they had the support of broad coalitions and diverse groups of voters. Through decades of campaigning, debating, and lobbying, western women won the right to vote. They used their experience and knowledge to support the expansion of women's rights across the country.

Through decades of campaigning, debating, and lobbying, western women won the right to vote. They used their experience and knowledge to support the expansion of women's rights across the country.

Ruth Asawa

Ruth Asawa was born in California in 1926. Her parents immigrated to the United States from Japan before her birth. Asawa's life was uprooted after Japan's attack on the American Naval Base in Pearl Harbor, Hawai'i in 1941. The US government declared war on Japan and forced all Japanese and Japanese Americans in the United States to relocate to internment camps. Even though Asawa was an American citizen, she was forcibly detained at the Rohwer War Relocation Center in Arkansas. She spent her teenage years confined at Rohwer until the end of World War II in 1945. While interned, Asawa studied art. Shortly after she was released, she enrolled at Black Mountain College in North Carolina.

Founded in 1933, the experimental Black Mountain College was internationally known for its modernist advancements in American art and education. Today, the Black Mountain College Historic District is listed on the National Register of Historic Places for its association with famous artists like Asawa.

The college provided opportunities for women and people of color to learn and express their creativity. Even though schools in the South were still segregated, African Americans like Mary Parks Washington felt welcome at Black Mountain. During her time at the school, Washington roomed with Asawa and the two became lifelong friends. Washington went on to teach art classes to elementary school students.

View from steps of Black Mountain College, ca. 1939. Black Mountain, North Carolina.

Asawa spent three years at Black Mountain and became a noted sculptor. She is famous for her intricate wire sculptures and her work has been displayed at galleries across the United States and Europe.

Associated Places:
Black Mountain College Historic District, Black Mountain, North Carolina (listed on the National Register of Historic Places).

Rohwer War Relocation Center Cemetery, near Rohwer, Arkansas (listed on the National Register of Historic Places and designated a National Historic Landmark).

—Katherine Crawford-Lackey

Located on Eden Lake, the Bauhaus-style building known as "The Ship" was built in 1941. It was designed by A. Lawrence Kocher, a professor at Black Mountain College. The building once served as the Studies Building. Today it is part of Camp Rockmont for Boys.

First Congregational Church in Portland, ca. 1892.

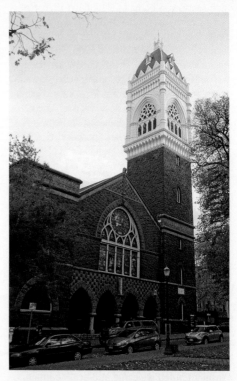

First Congregational Church in Portland, contemporary photograph.

In the summer of 1905, the National American Woman Suffrage Association (NAWSA) held its 37th annual meeting in Portland, Oregon. NAWSA leaders arranged for the meeting to coincide with the Lewis and Clark Centennial Exposition taking place in Portland. The exposition commemorated the one hundredth anniversary of the famous expedition. Drawing crowds from across the country, it featured exhibits, rides, and concerts.

That June, suffragists from Virginia, New York, Connecticut, Iowa, Illinois, and many other states attended the meeting. Even 85 year-old Susan B. Anthony made the trip to Portland. Despite her advanced age, Anthony felt it was important to take part in the yearly gathering. It was to be her last as she died less than a year later.

On most days, suffragists met at the First Congregational Church, now listed in the National Register of Historic Places. National leaders such as Anthony, Dr. Anna Howard Shaw,

Lewis and Clark Exposition in Portland, Oregon, 1905. Exhibit of Linn Company, Oregon in the Agriculture Palace.

and Carrie Chapman Catt gave rousing speeches. Many local politicians also pledged their support for women's suffrage.

Suffragists also attended the Lewis and Clark Exposition. The exposition organizers planned a ceremony to unveil a statue in tribute to Sacagawea, the Native American woman who guided Lewis and Clark on their journey. Anthony gave the opening remarks at the ceremony, acknowledging the importance of women in America. The exposition also featured a "Woman's Day" that many of the suffragists attended.

NAWSA's presence in Portland helped generate support from local politicians. It also inspired many Oregon women to establish their own suffrage organizations.

Lewis and Clark Exposition, 1905. Balloon ascension over Guild's Lake.

Associated Places:
First Congregational Church, Portland, Oregon (listed on the National Register of Historic Places)

Lewis and Clark National Historic Trail (approximately 4,900 miles long, it runs through 16 states from Pittsburgh, Pennsylvania to the mouth of the Columbia river, near what is now Astoria, Oregon)

—Katherine Crawford-Lackey

Front Entrance of the Lewis and Clark Exposition, 1905.

Woman Suffrage in the Midwest

by Elyssa Ford

Unlike other regions of the country where it is possible to see clear patterns in the woman suffrage story, such as the West with its early successes or the South where racism impeded the expansion of voting rights, the Midwest has no single dominant narrative of the woman suffrage campaign. When the Nineteenth Amendment passed in 1920, all Midwestern states had extended some form of suffrage to women but few granted women full voting rights. Several others offered women presidential and municipal suffrage, others allowed presidential suffrage alone. While two states had approved woman suffrage measures in the early 1910s, most of these states acted only shortly before the federal amendment passed.[1]

Despite such variation, there were several common threads in the midwestern fight for woman suffrage. The values of piety, morality, and domesticity led to strong and complicated ties to other social movements. Issues of race, ethnicity, and class as well as the rural-urban divide created internal divisions. They also provided opportunities for expanded support. At times midwestern suffragists found themselves at odds with the national leadership, even as they sometimes depended on them for guidance and financial support. These threads demonstrate why suffrage success was difficult, though not impossible, to achieve in these states.

Discussion of woman suffrage first began in the Midwest's eastern states as suffragists from the East toured the region. In 1845 and 1846, Ernestine Rose of New York campaigned for social reform and women's rights. She even spoke in the hall of the Michigan House of Representatives on these controversial issues.[2] In 1853, Lucy Stone, an organizer from Massachusetts, began a speaking tour of what she called "the West"—Ohio, Kentucky, Indiana, Missouri, Illinois, and Wisconsin. Even in her radical bloomer outfit, she received a warm welcome in these midwestern states. In St. Louis, the newspaper reported that her talk drew the largest crowd ever assembled for a speaker. A medical college suspended classes so faculty and students could attend, and a local minister even cancelled the Christmas Eve service so that the congregation could hear Stone's lecture instead.[3]

At times midwestern suffragists found themselves at odds with the national leadership, even as they sometimes depended on them for guidance and financial support. These threads demonstrate why suffrage success was difficult, though not impossible, to achieve in these states.

Midwestern women began to organize local suffrage societies and campaigns in the 1860s and 1870s, after the disruption of the Civil War. One of the first was the Missouri Suffrage Association, founded in 1867. In that same year, supporters of both Black and woman suffrage organized the Impartial Suffrage Association in Kansas. The purpose was to fight for two proposed amendments to the state constitution, one to strike "white" and another to strike "male" from the state's voting requirements. The brutal campaign ended up pitting supporters of African American and woman suffrage against one another. In the end, the electorate defeated both amendments.[4] Soon, other state legislatures and constitutional conventions across the Midwest also considered the question of woman suffrage. At times success was achingly close, but all failed. In 1870 Michigan legislators approved woman suffrage, only for the measure to be vetoed by the governor. In 1872 woman suffrage lost by a single vote in the Dakota Territory.[5] By that time, women in most midwestern states had created their own statewide societies to support these suffrage efforts.[6]

Like other regions of the country, the Midwest faced the challenge of trying to coordinate the various suffrage groups. In many states, local and state organizing

Five women from the Minnesota branch of the Congressional Union stand with their banners in front of the National Woman's Party headquarters in DC. One of the banners attests to the involvement of Scandinavian women in the suffrage movement.

Throughout their fight for the vote, one constant remained. Midwestern suffrage groups, much like those in the East, focused on morality, piety, and domesticity. These were the values women promised to bring to the political arena.

preceded national campaigns. While national groups saw themselves as directing the suffrage movement from above, in many ways national organizing was a response to preexisting grassroots efforts. The national organizations at times struggled to influence state campaigns as state and local organizations tried to remain independent.[7] For instance, when divisions led to the separate formation of the American Woman Suffrage Association (AWSA) from the National Woman Suffrage Association (NWSA) in 1869, the Missouri Suffrage Association refused to join either group. Later, the Missouri organization became badly divided by affiliations with both AWSA and NWSA. Iowa formed its first state-level organization in 1870. Despite the presence of national representatives from both groups, they decided to remain independent. Just a year later, the Indiana Woman Suffrage Association chose to withdraw from AWSA and become independent.[8]

Tensions between national, state, and local suffragists came to the fore in Michigan in 1874. In that year, the question of woman suffrage was sent to male voters. Susan B. Anthony increasingly believed that state strategies like this hurt the national effort but still decided to go to Michigan. To her surprise, she received an unenthusiastic welcome. Local suffrage workers were concerned that Anthony's ties to the controversial "free love" advocate Victoria Woodhull would provide fodder for anti-suffragists. Even newspapers traditionally in support of woman suffrage wrote attack articles about Anthony and Woodhull. They condemned the outside, eastern presence and their immoral values. In the end, suffrage lost by a vote of 135,000 to 40,000. Local organizers blamed Anthony and other national leaders for tainting the campaign. National groups blamed local suffragists for being poorly organized.[9]

Despite these tensions, many midwestern suffragists were leaders in the national movement. Unsuccessful in securing the vote through state legislatures and constitutional conventions, midwestern suffragists pioneered a strategy that became known as the New Departure. In 1869 at a national suffrage convention in St. Louis, Virginia Minor and her husband, Francis, pointed to the Fourteenth Amendment to argue that women, as citizens, already had the right to vote. In answer to the Minors' call for women to simply use this right, hundreds of women across the country went to the polls. Most were denied and some, including Susan B. Anthony, were arrested. In 1872, Virginia Minor sued after she was refused voter registration in Missouri. *Minor v. Happersett* advanced to the US Supreme Court, which ruled unanimously that voting was not a right of citizenship. This seminal case ended the New Departure and forced suffragists to redouble their efforts on state legislatures and a national amendment.[10]

Throughout their fight for the vote, one constant remained. Midwestern suffrage groups, much like those in the East, focused on morality, piety, and domesticity. These were the values women promised to bring to the political arena.[11] As one male Iowa state senator said in support of woman suffrage in 1865, "Do you want all grogshops, gambling houses, and corrupt houses of ill-fame banished from the State? If so, let women vote. They will elect men who will execute the laws, and legislators who will enact laws."[12] Yet this emphasis on morality proved to be problematic. The Woman's Christian Temperance Union (WCTU) was founded in 1874 in Cleveland, Ohio, a city known as "the Mecca of the Crusade" against alcohol. Under president Frances Willard's "Do Everything" campaign, unveiled in 1882, the WCTU encouraged members to support woman suffrage. This made the WCTU an important ally of the suffrage movement. However, suffragists' alignment with the WCTU also created powerful enemies.[13]

The liquor industry actively opposed the temperance movement and, through extension, voting rights for women. Wisconsin brewers provided the nation's best funded opposition to woman suffrage.[14] The German-American Alliance also was hostile to woman suffrage because of its connection to the brewing industry. By 1914 the alliance had a membership in the millions and a powerful lobby in Washington.[15] Germans provided significant opposition to suffrage throughout the Midwest. Other ethnic groups also aligned with liquor interests. At the 1880 Democratic convention in South Dakota, a large delegation of Russian immigrants wore liquor industry badges that proclaimed "Against Woman Suffrage and Susan B. Anthony."[16]

A particularly crushing defeat at the hands of the liquor industry came in Michigan in 1912. After decades of organizing, the governor called for a vote. The measure had strong support from various interests, including farmers. Victory seemed assured until alcohol lobbyists pressed for a recount. There was a strong suspicion of ballot tampering during that process, and suffrage lost by seven hundred votes. Women in Michigan had to wait until 1917 for presidential suffrage and 1918 for full suffrage.[17]

As suffragists realized the problems that came with their relationship with prohibitionists, they moved away from working closely with the temperance movement. In South Dakota, suffrage proponents ended their alliance

In some areas it was the passage of state prohibition laws that finally allowed woman suffrage to gain traction because only then did the opposition from the liquor industry cease.

Following decades of defeat in Nebraska, urban-based suffrage organizations changed their approach in 1914 and included rural women in their push.

with temperance advocates in the mid-1910s. They also began sending the German community copies of their suffrage paper.[18] Still, the association between temperance and woman suffrage lingered. In some areas it was the passage of state prohibition laws that finally allowed woman suffrage to gain traction because only then did the opposition from the liquor industry cease. Following a divisive and ultimately unsuccessful battle for suffrage in Kansas in 1867, proponents were hopeful following the passage of state prohibition in 1879. With that success, the WCTU held significant influence in the state. Their ties to the Kansas Equal Suffrage Association helped lead to passage of the country's first state-level municipal woman suffrage law in 1887.[19] Something similar happened in South Dakota. In 1916 men in the state voted on both prohibition and woman suffrage. Prohibition won while woman suffrage garnered 48 percent of the vote, an unprecedented high. Suffrage supporters believed their success was now assured because the liquor vote had been silenced. They were right; at their next attempt, in 1918, South Dakota women finally achieved full suffrage.[20]

Midwestern suffragists adopted arguments of female morality, piety, and domesticity as justifications for the vote beyond their connection with temperance. Jane Addams promoted a variation of this argument with her call for municipal housekeeping (also called civic or public housekeeping). Drawing upon her experience with settlement houses in Chicago, Addams did not argue that women were different from men and, thus, could purify politics. Instead she argued that women's household tasks actually made them uniquely qualified to be city leaders and to clean up the problems caused by industrialization. "The ballot," she said, "would afford the best possible protection to working women and expedite that protective legislation which they so sadly need and in which America is so deficient."[21]

Addams's argument resonated best in the region's cities, such as Chicago, Omaha, Minneapolis, and St. Louis, where most suffrage activities were centered. But midwestern states also had significant rural populations with somewhat different concerns. Organizations like the Grange, Farmers' Alliance, and Populist Party routinely endorsed woman suffrage in the Midwest. By the 1890s, suffrage groups became more adept at leveraging that support. This was especially true in Kansas where these rural associations all promoted the role of women within their organizations and supported a more democratic and egalitarian society. In 1892, shortly after the founding of the Populist Party in Kansas, rural publications targeted women as farmers and as political actors. Its paper, the *Farmer's Wife*, declared a "Women's War" and vowed to fight any suffrage opponents until the vote was won.[22]

Leaders in other states also targeted farm women with their publications and grassroots campaigns. Following decades of defeat in Nebraska, urban-based suffrage organizations changed their approach in 1914 and included rural women in their push. They wrote articles that targeted farm wives and specifically asked their opinions. They even expanded their donation policy to accept crops and farm animals to encourage rural involvement. The message was received positively. As one rural woman wrote to a suffrage paper, "The woman farm owner is considered a citizen only when the taxes fall due, but on election day she may not say how those taxes are spent." Despite their differences, rural and urban Nebraska women were able to see that they both were without an important voice—the vote. Nebraska suffragists' ability to broaden their message to include rural areas helped them win partial suffrage in 1918.[23]

Something similar happened in Iowa. In the late nineteenth century, urban suffrage leaders preferred to work within their own social circles. When their efforts garnered few results, they looked to new ways to attract rural support. These included an automobile tour of small communities and speakers on the Chautauqua circuit. In 1916, with this dual urban-rural approach, suffragists undertook one of the largest grassroots campaigns in Iowa's history. The vote for the suffrage referendum failed in the end. But the change in tactic contributed to a closer vote than previous ones in 1872 and 1909.[24]

The organizing and mobilizing by the region's African American women also contributed to suffrage successes. At times Black women were supported by white suffrage leaders. For instance, when Lucy Stone learned that Black women had been denied entrance to her talk in Indiana while on her 1853 tour of the Midwest, she demanded that African Americans be permitted to attend the following night. She was steadfast in her decision even when told this would mean some of the local white population would refuse to attend.[25] More frequently, it was Black women who had to demand that white suffragists include their voices and perspectives. Josephine St. Pierre did this at the 1900 meeting of the General Federation of Women's Clubs in Wisconsin when

Ida B. Wells-Barnett formed the Alpha Suffrage Club in January 1913 for African American women in the Chicago area. The club sent Wells-Barnett to the national suffrage parade in DC in early March that same year. By the publication of this article in November, the group had over one hundred members, and by 1915 its membership had reached two hundred.

FRAGE

ERS.

HIO!

ARE DEAL

September 3 – 1912.

E IN AND LEARN

HY WOMEN

GHT to Vote.

Woman suffrage headquarters, Upper Euclid Avenue, Cleveland, 1912. Some of the earliest women's rights conventions were held in Ohio, and the American Woman Suffrage Association was established in Cleveland in 1869. Despite this, suffrage amendments to the Ohio constitution were voted down repeatedly, and women there did not gain full suffrage until 1920 with the ratification of the Nineteenth Amendment.

she pushed for Black and white women to unify. Instead, she was taunted. Other leading Black women, such as Mary Church Terrell from the National Association of Colored Women, were not even allowed to speak.[26] Often excluded from white women's suffrage meetings, Black women organized among themselves to advance suffrage rights for all African Americans. Even though Black women in the Midwest did not face the same hostility as those in the South, they still endured discrimination within the suffrage movement.

Once they gained suffrage, Black women proved to be an influential voting bloc. Illinois women gained local suffrage in 1914, and Black leaders such as Ida B. Wells-Barnett immediately began to mobilize Black women as voters. This was partly because they feared that the state planned to offer broader suffrage but only to white women. Wells wanted to ensure that Black women were aware of their rights. They had largely been left out of the Illinois Woman Suffrage Association, but due to Wells's work and the potential threat to their voting rights, Black women created the Alpha Suffrage Club. They gained the support of Black men by arguing that they wanted the vote to help elect Black men into office. Through their efforts to register men and women, Chicago's predominately Black Second Ward soon was sixth out of the city's thirty-five wards for voter registration. The Alpha Suffrage Club then put those voters to work. The group helped elect the city's first

Black alderman and defeat a candidate supported by white suffragists. Black women also demonstrated the power of their collective action in Ohio. In 1919, the Colored Women's Republican Club changed its name to the Colored Women's Independent Political League. This was a public repudiation of that party when the Republican-dominated Ohio legislature defeated an equal rights bill. This successful work by Black women made other groups take notice. Anti-suffragists in the South used the Illinois example to demonstrate the danger of extending the vote and, thereby, expanding Black voting potential.[27]

By the start of the twentieth century, the national woman suffrage movement had come together with the creation of the National American Woman Suffrage Association (NAWSA) in 1890, which united NWSA and AWSA. Yet new divisions appeared with the formation of the more radical Congressional Union in 1913. Its leader Alice Paul quickly began to make movements into the Midwest. She was met with varied responses. The Ohio Woman Suffrage Association invited both NAWSA and the Congressional Union to set up offices in the state in 1915. Carrie Chapman Catt of Iowa, president of NAWSA,

said that the Ohio group had "lost its senses." She urged the state to oppose the Congressional Union. Leaders in Wisconsin and Minnesota also called for an end to the divisions and tried to work with both national groups.[28] Despite the national divisions, groups in the Midwest— just as they had earlier with AWSA and NWSA—often wanted to see less fighting and more collaboration.

By 1915, ten western states and Kansas—the first in the Midwest—had adopted full woman suffrage.[29] Successful on their third attempt in 1912, Kansas suffragists adopted a wide range of tactics. They held bazaars and teas to raise money and worked with local communities to stage the play *How the Vote Was Won*. They also held essay contests in public schools, where children competed for prizes but the real purpose was to convert their parents to the suffrage cause. With a margin of almost twenty thousand votes, Kansas became "the seventh star" of woman suffrage in the country and the first in the Midwest.[30]

Throughout this period, national speakers continued to travel the Midwest. In 1914, Alice Paul sent Congressional Union organizers to the states with full suffrage. Paul's goal was to organize women and men to support a federal suffrage amendment and to vote against Democratic candidates as a means of opposing the party's anti-suffrage tendencies. One organizer reported from Kansas that she was well-received in the state. She shared accounts that, upon hearing her message, people were planning to change their life-long affiliation with the Democratic Party. Despite this push, Democratic presidential candidate Woodrow Wilson won reelection in 1916 in almost all of the suffrage states, including Kansas.[31]

The Congressional Union—by 1917 known as the National Woman's Party (NWP)—was disappointed with its two-year effort. By 1918 the NWP was doing limited on-the-ground work in the Midwest. Their few scattered speaking tours, according to the speakers, had little impact in a region that seemed to be without hope. That year, Alice Henkle, an NWP representative, wrote home to the organization's headquarters, "I hope this is my last week here. Kansas City [Missouri] is the limit, but I hope I am bringing something out of the chaos I found here. At least we have a lot of activity and that has stirred up the women to really take an interest."[32]

The reality of the suffrage push in Missouri—like in much of the Midwest—was stronger and more active than Alice Henkle understood. After early initial success in the West, suffragists won no new states between

As suffragists realized the problems that came with their relationship with prohibitionists, they moved away from working closely with the temperance movement.

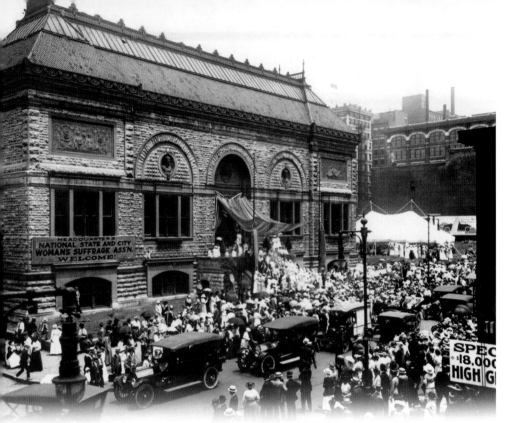

1896 and 1910. Then, in the short time from 1910 to 1916, they achieved victories across the West and in Kansas. They organized intensely throughout the region in that period, with referenda in Ohio, Wisconsin, Michigan, North and South Dakota, Missouri, and Nebraska.[33] These votes failed, but suffragists in Michigan and South Dakota soon achieved their goal with the passage of full suffrage in 1918. By 1919 all other midwestern states extended partial suffrage to women. Though not as successful as their sisters in the West, suffragists in the Midwest achieved extraordinary victories despite organized and powerful opposition. They led almost constant suffrage campaigns and adeptly changed their tactics as circumstances dictated. Through signature gathering, parades, automobile tours, theatric tableaus, speeches, tabling at county fairs, and publications, suffragists in the Midwest worked within their local communities, struggled to bridge the rural-urban divide, allied with friendly political parties and organizations, devised strategies to counter their well-funded opposition, and drew guidance and inspiration from national organizations. These diverse approaches made the Midwest one of the most varied and successful regions in the country in the campaign for woman suffrage.

In June 1916, more than three thousand women, clad in white, held a "walkless, talkless parade" in St. Louis, Missouri. They lined the streets and forced the all-male delegates to the Democratic National Convention to walk past them en route to the convention. The goal was to demonstrate how, without the vote, the voices of women had been silenced.

Woman Suffrage in New England

by Heather Munro Prescott

An examination of the history of woman suffrage in New England uncovers examples of critical suffrage activism on the state and local level. It also demonstrates how suffragists from the region helped build the suffrage cause into a national movement.

Many histories of woman suffrage use the 1848 convention in Seneca Falls, New York as a starting point for the movement. But New York State was not the only place women fought for the right to vote during the mid-nineteenth century. Women and men from the New England states of Maine, Vermont, New Hampshire, Massachusetts, Connecticut, and Rhode Island also mobilized for women's rights in the 1840s. Because Susan B. Anthony and Elizabeth Cady Stanton's published history of the suffrage movement emphasized Seneca Falls and downplayed or even left out suffragists from other parts of the country, the significance of the New England region in the national suffrage campaign has been neglected.[1] An examination of the history of woman suffrage in New England uncovers examples of critical suffrage activism on the state and local level. It also demonstrates how suffragists from the region helped build the suffrage cause into a national movement.

As in other parts of the country, the women's rights movement in New England grew out of efforts to abolish slavery. In 1847, noted female abolitionists Angelina and Sarah Grimké toured New England and staunchly defended a woman's right to speak out against slavery in public. The Grimké sisters persuaded women and men from the region to join the fight against slavery. They also inspired a small number of New England women to use the abolitionist cause as a platform for advancing the rights of women.[2]

New England's most notable early suffragist was Lucy Stone of Massachusetts. Ten years after the Grimké's toured the region, Stone delivered her first lecture on behalf of women's rights at her brother's church in Gardner, Massachusetts. Soon after, she moved to Boston to begin a position as a paid lecturer for the Massachusetts Anti-Slavery Society. Stone enraged some audiences by daring to criticize women's lack of rights alongside her condemnation of slavery. Declaring, "I was a woman before I was an abolitionist," Stone defended her actions.[3] Stone's renown as a speaker soon extended beyond New England. Following the 1848 women's rights convention in Seneca Falls, Elizabeth Cady Stanton suggested that convention organizers enlist Stone as a national lecturer on women's rights.

Although no one took up this proposition, Stone, along with Stanton and Susan B. Anthony, soon became among the most prominent suffrage leaders in the country.[4]

In 1850, Stone and several other New England women, including Abby Kelley Foster of Massachusetts and Paulina Wright Davis of Rhode Island, organized the first national women's rights convention in Worcester, Massachusetts. They wanted to see if they could generate support for suffrage around the country. Nearly one thousand men and women from eleven states attended. All but two of the attendees were native-born, white Protestants. The exceptions were Sojourner Truth, a former slave and prominent abolitionist, and Ernestine Rose, a Jewish immigrant from Poland. In an impassioned speech, Foster declared women had the same duty to rise up against tyranny as their ancestors had against King George III. In 1851, another national convention held in Worcester drew an even larger audience.[5] These meetings, along with lectures by Stone and other suffrage leaders, inspired women throughout the nation to organize their own local efforts on behalf of women's rights.[6]

Lucy Stone of Massachusetts, November 1853.

Like their counterparts elsewhere, women's rights activists in New England put their cause on hold during the Civil War. After the war, they resumed their activism and began planning the formation of a regional suffrage organization. In 1868, they founded the New England Woman Suffrage Association (NEWSA). They named noted poet and author Julia Ward Howe, best known for writing "The Battle Hymn of the Republic," president, and Lucy Stone a member of the executive committee. Other founding members included Paulina Wright Davis of Rhode Island and Isabelle Beecher Hooker of Connecticut.[7]

The NEWSA soon became embroiled in the national debate over the Fifteenth Amendment to the US Constitution. This amendment would prohibit denying the franchise based on "race, color, or previous condition of servitude." One of the founders of the NEWSA, Olympia Brown, favored Anthony and Stanton's insistence that woman suffrage be pursued alongside the enfranchisement of African American men. But Howe declared she would not demand the vote for herself until the freedman first obtained that right. Stone disagreed with Frederick Douglass's claim that "the cause of the negro was more pressing than that of woman's." She nevertheless agreed that Black male suffrage should come first.[8]

The NEWSA formed the basis of the American Woman Suffrage Association (AWSA). It was founded in 1869 as an alternative to the National Women's Suffrage Association (NWSA) led by Stanton and Anthony. Unlike the NWSA, the AWSA protested both gender-based and race-based discrimination and prioritized the struggle for Black male suffrage. In order to avoid putting the fight for woman suffrage in direct conflict with Black suffrage, the AWSA abandoned efforts to include woman suffrage in the same constitutional amendment as Black suffrage. Instead, it focused its efforts on changing state laws that prohibited women from voting. Only when Black men had the right to vote would the AWSA seek a separate constitutional amendment for woman suffrage.[9]

This schism between the AWSA and the NWSA continued even after passage of the Fifteenth Amendment in 1870. The two organizations disagreed primarily over political strategies. The NWSA insisted that an amendment to the US Constitution was the best way to achieve woman suffrage. The AWSA, on the other hand, argued that Congress would not support woman suffrage until a critical number of states had granted women the right to vote. The AWSA encouraged the growth of state organizations that would campaign for woman suffrage on a state-by-state basis. Stone and her husband, Henry Blackwell, also created the weekly newspaper the *Woman's Journal*. It served as the AWSA's the principal means of communicating with affiliated state organizations.[10]

Stanton and Anthony considered the state-based tactic foolhardy. Leaving woman suffrage to the states, Stanton argued, would "defer indefinitely its settlement."[11] Nevertheless, most women from New England agreed with the AWSA strategy. They formed their own state organizations to pressure their respective legislatures to extend the vote to women. Since most New Englanders considered the education of children and youth to be within

The NEWSA formed the basis of the American Woman Suffrage Association (AWSA). It was founded in 1869 as an alternative to the National Women's Suffrage Association (NWSA) led by Stanton and Anthony.

women's proper sphere, New England suffrage activists were most successful in campaigns for school suffrage and for the right of women to sit on school boards and to elect its members. New Hampshire was the first to approve school suffrage for women, in 1878, followed by the other New England states in the next few years.[12]

New England suffragists used the argument of "social housekeeping"—that women would clean up urban politics and social ills—to make a case for allowing women to vote in municipal elections. Frequently these campaigns for municipal suffrage drew on anti-immigrant and anti-Catholic bigotry. In Massachusetts, for example, anti-immigrant Republican men believed that native-born Protestant women would be more likely to vote than Catholic women, who would be discouraged from voting by their husbands. Thus, woman suffrage would save the state from "rum and Romanism" by diluting the Catholic vote and promoting the cause of temperance. Despite these appeals, the Republican Party as a whole did not support municipal suffrage for women. The Democratic Party, especially its Irish Catholic wing, which linked woman suffrage to nativism, temperance, and anti-family radicalism. They also opposed enfranchising women.[13]

Vermont was the only New England state to grant women the right to vote in municipal elections. The municipal suffrage campaign in the Green Mountain State was successful largely because, as a rural state, Vermont lacked a sizable urban immigrant population to mount an anti-suffrage attack. On the other hand, the temperance movement, considered an appropriate political cause for women to embrace, was extremely popular in the state. Vermont suffragists convinced state legislators that female voters would help make the state dry. In 1917, the Vermont state legislature approved granting women the right to vote in municipal elections.[14]

The work of New England suffragists eventually contributed to a rapprochement between the AWSA and the NWSA. Lucy Stone's daughter, Alice Stone Blackwell, was instrumental in unifying the competing national suffrage organizations. Negotiations between Blackwell, representing the AWSA, and Rachel Foster, of the NWSA, led to the formation of the National American Woman Suffrage Association (NAWSA) in 1890. The new organization elected Stanton president, Anthony vice president, Stone chair of executive committee, and Blackwell corresponding secretary. The *Woman's Journal* became NAWSA's official publication and remained based in Boston. NAWSA retained the AWSA strategy of campaigning for woman suffrage on a state-by-state basis. Although this tactic had

New England suffragists used the argument of "social housekeeping"—that women would clean up urban politics and social ills—to make a case for allowing women to vote in municipal elections.

Massachusetts suffragists distributing the *Woman's Journal and Suffrage News* in Boston, November 1913. The *Woman's Journal* was the official publication of the National American Woman's Suffrage Association.

limited success in New England, it led to a number of suffrage victories in the far and middle West. This strategy also reinvigorated state and regional suffrage organizations in New England and other areas of the country.[15]

Julia Ward Howe expressed concern that the merger would lead to the abandonment of the AWSA's commitment to racial equality. Howe's fears proved correct: NAWSA dedicated itself solely to woman suffrage. It also adopted a racist and nativist strategy of "educated suffrage." They argued that educated, usually white and native-born women were more deserving of the vote than "ignorant" Black and immigrant men. Although educated suffrage could, theoretically, include the small number of educated Black women in the country, white suffrage organizations excluded or marginalized Black women.[16]

During the 1890s, middle-class Black women founded their own organizations dedicated to fighting both gender and race discrimination. Among the leaders in this endeavor was Josephine Ruffin of Boston. She was founder of the city's Woman's Era Club and the monthly newsletter the *Woman's Era*. It was dedicated to providing a venue for "intercourse and sympathy" for women of all races but especially "the educated and refined, among the colored women." The pages of the *Woman's Era* expressed strong support for Ida B. Wells' campaign against lynching and chastised NAWSA for its tacit support of white supremacy. In 1895, the Woman's Era Club organized a convention in Boston for representatives from Black women's clubs around the nation. Attendees created the Federation of African-American Women, forerunner of the National Association of Colored Women (NACW). The NACW established a woman suffrage department to educate members about the suffrage cause. It received no support from NAWSA, which continued its policy of ignoring and refusing aid to Black suffragists.[17]

NAWSA and its regional affiliates did reach out to white working-class women in an effort to expand its membership and win the support of white working-class male voters. This cross-class alliance was epitomized by the creation of the Women's Trade Union League (WTUL) at the American Federation of Labor's national convention in Boston in 1903. The WTUL elected Mary Morton Kimbell Kehew, a wealthy woman from Boston and descendant of a former Massachusetts governor, president and Mary Kenney O'Sullivan, an Irish Catholic labor organizer and resident of Denison Settlement House in Boston, secretary and first vice president. O'Sullivan's leadership was instrumental in persuading working-class men to support the suffrage cause. The WTUL dedicated itself to improving pay and working

Suffragist Helena Hill Weed of Norwalk, Connecticut, shown serving a three-day sentence in a Washington, DC, prison for carrying a banner that read "Governments derive their just powers from the consent of the governed."

conditions for women workers. It served as an umbrella organization for other women's trade unions. Its goals aligned perfectly with the social housekeeping mission of the mainstream suffrage movement. The WTUL established a suffrage department in 1908 and urged working women and their male allies to attend suffrage rallies.[18]

During the 1910s, some suffragists renewed demands for a federal amendment to the US Constitution granting women the right to vote. In 1913, Alice Paul and Lucy Burns took over the Congressional Committee of NAWSA, which they renamed the Congressional Union. Paul and Burns soon alienated NAWSA with their militant tactics. Most egregious was their proposal to campaign against Democratic candidates in the western states in order to pressure Congress and President Woodrow Wilson into supporting the suffrage amendment. NAWSA expelled the Congressional Union from the organization in 1914, and Burns and Paul formed the National Woman's Party in 1916.[19]

The National Woman's Party had local chapters in all of the New England states except Vermont. It is unclear why Vermont did not have a chapter. It is likely that the population of the state was too small to accommodate two suffrage organizations. Members of the state chapters of the National Woman's Party sent representatives to Washington to lobby Congress to pass the federal suffrage amendment. They also participated in the various parades and demonstrations organized by the National Woman's Party, including the pickets of the White House during

Connecticut suffragist Catherine M. Flanagan (left) being placed under arrest for picketing with banners at the White House East Gate, August 17, 1917. Flanagan and other picketers were sentenced to thirty days in Occoquan Workhouse. The banner reads "How Long Must Women Wait for Liberty?"

1918 and 1919. Thirty suffragists from New England were charged with "obstructing traffic" and sentenced to prison. While there, they endured deplorable living conditions and mistreatment by guards.[20]

Katherine Houghton Hepburn, president of the Connecticut Woman Suffrage Association (CWSA), disagreed with the tactics of the NWP but also praised its dedication to the suffrage cause. In an interview with the *Hartford Courant*, Hepburn expressed her support for Catharine Flanagan, who was arrested in August 1917: "I admire Mrs. Flanagan very much for being willing to go to jail for her convictions. It is more than most people could conceive of doing for an ideal."[21] This was markedly different from the position of NAWSA, which denounced the picketers as un-American. The organization threw its support behind President Wilson and the war effort. When NAWSA refused to condemn the horrific treatment of suffragists in prison, several leaders of the CWSA, including Hepburn, resigned from their offices in protest.[22]

The work of suffragists on the local and national level paid off. President Wilson urged Congress in 1918 to support woman suffrage as a war measure. Afterwards, suffragists around the country lobbied intensively to persuade their representatives and senators to follow through and pass a suffrage amendment. On January 10, 1918, Congresswoman Jeannette Rankin of Montana introduced the Nineteenth Amendment on the floor of the House of Representatives. The House passed the amendment the same day 274–136, just over the two-thirds majority required. The Senate voted the following day but fell two votes short of the necessary two-thirds. Although the majority of Republican senators voted in favor of the amendment, the Republican senators from Massachusetts—Henry Cabot Lodge and John Weeks—voted no. NAWSA and the National Woman's Party joined forces to target Weeks and three other senators who had voted against the amendment for defeat in the November 1918 election. The efforts of the Massachusetts Woman Suffrage Association contributed to the unseating of Weeks. He was replaced by Democrat David Walsh, a former governor and the first Democratic senator elected from Massachusetts in over a century. The following year, Senator Lodge attempted to delay a vote on the suffrage amendment on procedural grounds but failed. On June 4, 1919, the Senate passed the amendment, sending it to the states for ratification.[23]

President Wilson urged Congress in 1918 to support woman suffrage as a war measure. Afterwards, suffragists around the country lobbied intensively to persuade their representatives and senators to follow through and pass a suffrage amendment.

Four of the New England states contributed directly to ratifying the Nineteenth Amendment. Massachusetts was the eighth state in the nation to do so, in 1919. It was followed by New Hampshire and Maine the same year, and Rhode Island in 1920. Although Connecticut and Vermont were the thirty-seventh and thirty-eighth states to ratify the amendment, they were critical when the validity of the Tennessee and West Virginia votes were challenged in court. Plaintiff Oscar Leser sued the state of Maryland to prevent two women from voting in Baltimore. He charged, among other things, that the state legislatures in Tennessee and West Virginia had violated their rules of procedure in adopting the Nineteenth Amendment. In *Leser v. Garnett*, the US Supreme Court declared this point was moot. Since Connecticut and Vermont had ratified the amendment, the amendment had been ratified by enough states to become "valid to all intents and purposes as part of the Constitution of the United States."[24]

Although New England suffragists had limited success in gaining votes for women in their respective states, their political skills were critical in the push for a federal amendment to the US Constitution. Their story complicates the canonical history of woman suffrage that focuses on Seneca Falls. Several nationally prominent suffrage leaders hailed from the New England states, and the first two national women's rights conventions were held in Worcester, Massachusetts. From the mid-nineteenth century through to 1920, New England suffragists fought tirelessly for votes for women on the both the state and national level.

Although New England suffragists had limited success in gaining votes for women in their respective states, their political skills were critical in the push for a federal amendment to the US Constitution. Their story complicates the canonical history of woman suffrage that focuses on Seneca Falls.

Woman Suffrage in the Mid-Atlantic

by Christine L. Ridarsky

Women in the mid-Atlantic states were at the forefront of the woman suffrage movement at its inception in the mid-nineteenth century. They provided much of the leadership that would ultimately ensure ratification of the Nineteenth Amendment in 1920. A small band of mostly Quaker women, including Philadelphia's Lucretia Mott, along with Elizabeth Cady Stanton organized the first women's rights convention in Seneca Falls, New York, in 1848. Scholars have debated the true significance of this largely regional event. But these women inspired the national woman suffrage conventions that followed, held annually beginning in 1850—five in New York and one in Pennsylvania. These were arguably more influential in launching the women's movement prior to the Civil War.[1] In the twentieth century, a suffrage victory in New York and a push by Alice Paul and Lucy Burns for a national amendment finally helped make a woman suffrage amendment a reality.

Women's interest in securing their right to vote grew initially out of their experiences working for reform within antislavery and temperance circles. Their participation in these groups was limited by male leaders and social norms that prevented women from speaking publicly. Finding parallels between their own legal and social status and that of the enslaved, women's early efforts focused on achieving human and civil rights for Black men and all women. As a result, women in the Mid-Atlantic worked together across race lines early in the movement. Margaretta Forten and Harriet Forten Purvis, daughters of Black abolitionists James and Charlotte Forten, helped organize the fifth National Women's Rights Convention in Philadelphia in 1854. Black women likely attended most, if not all, of the early women's rights conventions, though the minutes usually did not record their presence.[2]

Lucretia Mott, ca. 1870-1880.

In addition to organizing the annual conventions, women's rights activism in the antebellum era included writing, lecturing, and petitioning legislators for change. In 1849, Amelia Bloomer started publishing the *Lily* in Seneca Falls. It was the first newspaper for women in the United States. Though it initially focused on temperance, Elizabeth Cady Stanton, writing under the alias "Sunflower," quickly pushed it into addressing broader women's rights themes.[3]

Women largely suspended their women's rights activism during the Civil War. They chose instead to focus on supporting soldiers and assisting formerly enslaved people who were freed by President Lincoln's Emancipation Proclamation. At the war's end, however, women immediately resumed their efforts to secure rights for African Americans and women. In 1866, as the nation debated the meaning of citizenship in the wake of emancipation, Elizabeth Cady Stanton, now living in New York City, and Susan B. Anthony, of Rochester, New York, established the New York Equal Rights Association as well as the American Equal Rights Association (AERA). These groups agitated for suffrage "irrespective of race, color or sex."[4] The AERA elected Mott its president, and Black and white activists continued to work side by side. Harriet Purvis served on the AERA's executive committee.[5] Other state affiliates soon organized. Philadelphia activists founded the Pennsylvania Equal Rights Association in January 1867. In October, women in Vineland, New Jersey, organized the Vineland Equal Rights Association. They sent a petition to the Republican state convention advocating for "Impartial Suffrage, irrespective of Sex or Color." New Jersey women also established one of the first US organizations dedicated specifically to securing the vote for women. In November 1867 they founded the New Jersey Woman Suffrage Association (NJWSA) and elected Lucy Stone, living in Orange, president and her sister -in-law, Antoinette Brown Blackwell, of Somerville, vice president.[6]

New York's 1867 constitutional convention provided an opportunity for the AERA to press its case for universal suffrage. Woman suffragists thought they had an ally in Suffrage Committee chairman Horace Greeley.

Harriet Forten Purvis, ca. 1874.

Susan B. Anthony and Elizabeth
Cady Stanton, n.d.

He had supported women's voting rights as editor of
the *New-York Tribune*. But when Greeley submitted his
report, he recommended amending the state constitution to give the vote to Black men but not women.
Angered at the betrayal, Stanton and Anthony attacked
the manhood of convention delegates who opposed
woman suffrage. The tactic backfired. Delegates voted
125 to 19 to support Greeley's position.[7] Ultimately, the
state's voters rejected the new constitution altogether
and enfranchised neither group.

New Jersey women also challenged voting restrictions. The original New Jersey constitution had allowed
women and Black men to vote, provided they met the
minimum requirement for property ownership. There is
evidence that at least a small number of women cast ballots
in the state's first decade. But in a dubious legal maneu-
ver, the legislature limited the vote to "free, white, male,
citizens" in 1807. The state constitution was amended in
1844 to reflect this change.[8] But after the Civil War women
began to assert their right to vote again. In March 1868,
Portia Kellogg Gage, a founder of the NJWSA, attempted
to vote in the local election in Vineland. She was turned
away because she was not registered.[9] In November, Gage
and 171 other women, Black and white, attempted to vote

in the federal election. When their ballots were refused, they set up their own table and their own special ballot box and proceeded to cast their votes. They continued this practice for several years.[10]

In 1869, debate over the Fifteenth Amendment, which prohibited denial of the vote on the basis of race, fractured the AERA, and the era of cross-racial alliances largely came to an end. Abolitionist Wendell Phillips declared it the "Negro's hour." He argued that women needed to temporarily set aside their demands for the benefit of the Black man. Stanton and Anthony refused.[11] Instead, they formed the National Woman Suffrage Association (NWSA) and focused on a national woman suffrage amendment. Lucy Stone and her husband, Henry Blackwell, set up the rival American Woman Suffrage Association (AWSA). It supported the Fifteenth Amendment and turned to state campaigns to secure voting rights for women. The NJWSA quickly aligned with the AWSA, as did the new Pennsylvania Woman Suffrage Association, established in December 1869 with abolitionist Mary Grew of Philadelphia as president.[12] The New York State Woman Suffrage Association, on the other hand, was organized nearly concurrent with the NWSA. For twenty years the two groups operated practically as one.

Almost immediately, suffragists focused on a federal approach adopted a strategy known as the New Departure. They argued that women had a legal right to vote based on language in the Fourteenth Amendment that defined citizens as "all persons born or naturalized in the United States." Contending that voting was one of the "privileges or immunities" of citizenship, women began to go to the polls.[13] After Philadelphia election officials refused to accept Carrie Burnham's ballot in 1871, she became one of the first to use the courts to test the argument. She relied not only on the Fourteenth Amendment but also on Pennsylvania law, which conferred voting rights on "freemen." Burnham argued that the term described status, not sex. The Pennsylvania Supreme Court disagreed, ruling against Burnham in 1873.[14] In November 1872, Susan B. Anthony was one of several Rochester women to cast her ballot in the presidential election. She was arrested. Anthony was charged with the crime of voting illegally and found guilty by a federal court. The judge decided the case on narrow grounds, leaving the constitutional question unsettled.[15] The US Supreme Court finally settled the matter of women's voting rights under the Fourteenth Amendment in 1875. It ruled in *Minor v. Happersett* that suffrage was not "one of the privileges or immunities of

In November 1872, Susan B. Anthony was one of several Rochester women to cast her ballot in the presidential election. She was arrested.

Rachel Foster Avery, 1887.

citizenship." States, therefore, had the right to exclude women from the franchise.[16]

Meanwhile, the AWSA and state suffrage societies focused on changing voting rights clauses in state constitutions. In 1873, Pennsylvania's constitutional convention acknowledged the requirements of the Fifteenth Amendment when it replaced the words "white freeman" with "male citizens." It specifically failed to include women. New York, New Jersey, and Delaware did not update their constitutions during this period.[17]

By 1876, the NWSA settled on a new strategy; it would seek an amendment to the US Constitution barring states from using sex as a basis for disenfranchisement. A proposed sixteenth amendment, later named for Susan B. Anthony, was introduced before Congress in 1878. It was largely buried in committee and ultimately defeated in 1887. With the federal strategy seemingly at an impasse, the rival NWSA and AWSA called a truce and merged to form the National American Woman Suffrage Association (NAWSA) in 1890. Anthony served as its first president and it was headquartered in New York City.

Now under a single umbrella, state suffrage organizations adopted a common strategy of organizing local and county suffrage clubs to disperse the suffrage message more broadly. The state associations in New York, New Jersey, and Pennsylvania all began encouraging formation of local and county affiliates. By 1893, New York's suffrage association reported that twenty-three auxiliary county clubs had been established.[18] Even women in Delaware began to organize. Under the leadership of Philadelphia's Rachel Foster Avery, a protégé of Susan B. Anthony, they established Delaware's first women's rights organization, the Wilmington Equal Suffrage Club, in November 1895.[19]

With constitutional conventions scheduled in New York in 1894 and Delaware in 1896, suffragists directed resources at those states throughout the 1890s. New York suffragists took a decidedly different tack than they had during the 1867 convention. Instead of "hanging about the convention" and lobbying delegates as they had in the earlier campaign, state president Jean Brooks Greenleaf determined that the best tactic was to organize a massive canvass to collect signatures on pro-suffrage petitions and calculate the value of taxable property owned by women. When the convention got underway in May 1894, suffragists presented petitions nearly every day for two weeks in support of striking the word "male" from the clause assigning voting rights. In August, the full convention debated the question over four days before voting ninety-seven to fifty-eight against woman suffrage.[20] In Delaware, women finally organized a state association in 1896. Despite their efforts, the woman suffrage amendment failed in Delaware's convention in 1897. The following year the legislature passed a law allowing taxpaying women to vote in school elections. New Jersey couldn't even get that much. In 1897, voters defeated an amendment that would have allowed women to vote in school elections.

The merger of the two national suffrage organizations came at a time of increasing racial tensions. These were marked by legalized segregation and violence against African Americans in the South and *de facto* segregation in the North. Black women found that they were no longer as welcome within mainstream suffrage organizations as they had once been. They set about establishing their own clubs, usually with broader objectives than those of their white counterparts. In Rochester, Hester C. Jeffrey founded several organizations for African American women, including the philanthropic and suffrage-focused Susan B. Anthony Club. Jeffrey also continued to work alongside her friend Susan B. Anthony within the New York State Woman Suffrage Association and NAWSA.[21] For Black women, the vote was about more than improving their own status. It was also about protecting the status of Black men who were being disenfranchised through educational tests and intimidation. Thus, few Black women's clubs were organized solely to advocate for suffrage, though many included it among the causes they supported.[22]

As Black women built their own movement, white activism seemed to plateau. Mainstream suffragists in mid-Atlantic states

Hester C. Jeffrey, ca. 1903.

Alice Paul, ca. 1913.

turned their attention to educating women about the benefits of equality rather than lobbying for legislative reform. But that changed early in the twentieth century as a new cadre of young leaders emerged. Anthony retired as NAWSA president in 1900 and died in 1906. Two of her acolytes led NAWSA over the next twenty years: Carrie Chapman Catt (1900–1905 and 1915–1920) and Anna Howard Shaw (1906–1914). Rachel Foster Avery reinvigorated the Pennsylvania movement when she was elected state president in 1908 and opened a headquarters in Philadelphia.[23] Elizabeth Cady Stanton's daughter Harriot Stanton Blatch also took on the mantle of leadership during this period. She established the Equality League of Self-Supporting Women, later the Women's Political Union, in New York City in 1907. Its goal was to draw working-class and immigrant women into what had been a predominantly middle-class Protestant movement.[24]

Among the most influential of these new twentieth-century leaders was Alice Paul, of Mount Laurel, New Jersey. Like Blatch, Paul had spent time in England learning the militant tactics of British suffragettes. She believed that American suffragists needed to take a more radical approach in pressing for their rights. This included organizing public spectacles to attract attention to the cause. In 1912, the annual New York City suffrage parade, inaugurated by Blatch in 1910, drew twenty-thousand marchers and half a million onlookers. Paul and colleague Lucy Burns, of New York, demonstrated another method for attracting attention when, in 1911, they staged the first open-air campaign in the Keystone State. With the help of Caroline Katzenstein, secretary of the Pennsylvania Woman Suffrage Association, they held twenty-one outdoor meetings across Philadelphia between July 25 and September 30.[25]

By 1913, Paul and Burns had formed the Congressional Union (CU), which grew out of NAWSA's Congressional Committee. The young militants clashed with the organization's more conservative leaders over strategy. NAWSA concentrated on winning the vote in the states, while Paul and Burns had returned to Stanton and Anthony's focus on a federal amendment. They argued that suffragists should hold the party in power (Democrats) publicly accountable.[26] They recruited Mabel Vernon to become their first national organizer, sending her first to her home state of Delaware to organize a state branch of the CU there.[27]

Carrie Chapman Catt, however, believed that Congress would never seriously consider amending the US Constitution until more states had changed their own voting laws. She set forth a plan for simultaneously seeking reform within individual states and at the federal level.

Beginning in 1909, Catt encouraged suffrage clubs to reorganize by legislative district in a manner similar to political parties.[28] The strategy was put to a test in 1915 when voters in New York, New Jersey, and Pennsylvania each voted for a referendum on woman suffrage. All were defeated. But Catt's "Winning Plan" finally paid off when New York State's voters granted full suffrage to women in November 1917. It was the first state east of the Mississippi River to do so. Catt declared that "the victory is not New York's alone. It's the nation's." She felt sure that Congress would now be forced to pass a federal amendment.[29] But as the United States entered World War I, NAWSA suspended most of its work. The National Woman's Party (NWP), however, which had grown out of the CU, refused to do so. They chose instead to use the war for freedom abroad to highlight the hypocrisy of women's disenfranchisement at home.

Beginning in January 1917, the NWP organized a series of protests outside the White House. "Silent Sentinels" held signs asking "Kaiser Wilson" how much longer women had to wait for equal rights, comparing the president to the German emperor. By spring 1919, when the pickets ended, more than 500 women had been arrested. Of these, 168 spent time in jail, including many mid-Atlantic women who were force fed during hunger strikes at the Occoquan Workhouse.[30]

Beginning in January 1917, the NWP organized a series of protests outside the White House. "Silent Sentinels" held signs asking "Kaiser Wilson" how much longer women had to wait for equal rights, comparing the president to the German emperor.

In June 1919, both houses of Congress passed the Nineteenth Amendment and sent it to the states for ratification. Thirty-six states needed to approve the measure. New York became the sixth state to ratify on June 16; Pennsylvanians approved the measure on June 24. New Jersey was slower to ratify but did so on February 10, 1920. By March, only one more state needed to ratify, and both NAWSA and the NWP looked to Delaware to put them over the top. But it wasn't to be. The state senate voted eleven to six for ratification, but in June the house refused to bring the measure to the floor, thereby killing it. Delaware wouldn't approve the amendment until March 1923, almost three years after the amendment took effect on August 26, 1919.

When Tennessee became the thirty-sixth state to ratify the Nineteenth Amendment, women throughout the nation secured the right to vote. The campaign that began in upstate New York in the 1840s came to an end. Mid-Atlantic women—from Lucretia Mott and Harriet Purvis, to Elizabeth Cady Stanton and Susan B. Anthony, to Alice Paul and Lucy Burns, and so many more—had been instrumental, as leaders and foot soldiers, in every aspect of the seventy-two-year battle for woman suffrage. It is hard to imagine the movement without them.

Suffragists and the Texas State Fair

Photo of modern-day Fair Park. Many of the buildings in the park today date to the 1936 Texas Centennial Exposition.

Grassroots organizing was a major part of women's effort to win the vote. Women across the country organized on the local level to win support for women's suffrage. The suffragists of Dallas, Texas were particularly skilled at organizing. They developed the unique strategy of leveraging social gatherings (parades, fairs, and festivals) to promote women's suffrage. They made sure to have a presence at important community events. One way they achieved this was by having a booth at the annual state fair.

The Texas State Fair first began in 1886 within the boundaries of what is now Fair Park, a National Historic Landmark District. The event drew crowds from all over the region. Attractions included horse races (and eventually automobile races), concerts, and farm equipment exhibitions. The women of the Dallas Equal Suffrage Association (DESA) also attended the fair.

From 1913 through 1917, the DESA set up a booth and spoke with fairgoers about the importance of women's suffrage. They also worked with fair organizers to host a "Suffrage Day" each year. On that day, the fair's official flag was a yellow and white banner embroidered with the words "Votes for Women." The DESA also hosted members of the Texas Equal Suffrage Association (TESA).

The 1915 State Fair was a particularly memorable event as hundreds of suffragists gathered for the cause. Both the DESA and TESA participated in the fair's automobile parade. They decorated their carriages and gave speeches from their vehicles.

Texas suffragists has a successful strategy for engaging their communities. Their efforts paid off, and the state of Texas ratified the Nineteenth Amendment on June 28, 1919.

Associated Places:
Fair Park, Dallas, Texas (designated a National Historic Landmark District).

The Fair Park Historic District includes the Hall of Administration, which from 2000 through 2011 housed The Women's Museum: An Institute for the Future.

—Katherine Crawford-Lackey

Woman Suffrage in the Southern States

by Sarah H. Case

The woman suffrage movement emerged later and had fewer victories in the South than in the West and Northeast. Regardless, southern women could claim responsibility for the decisive vote leading to the ratification of the Nineteenth Amendment to the Constitution, declaring that voting rights could not be restricted "on account of sex." In the summer of 1920, the amendment had passed Congress and been ratified by thirty-five of the necessary thirty-six states. All eyes turned to Tennessee. In August, the state senate easily ratified the amendment, but the vote in the house resulted in a tense tie. Surprising his colleagues, a young representative from a district with strong anti-suffrage support named Harry T. Burn suddenly changed his vote in favor of ratification. With Burn's vote, the woman suffrage amendment became part of the Constitution. When asked why he had changed his mind, Burn pointed to a letter from his mother. In it, she exhorted him to "vote for Suffrage and don't keep them in doubt . . . be a good boy and help Mrs. Catt [Carrie Chapman Catt, leader of the National American Suffrage Association] with her 'Rats.'!"[1]

This charming story of a loyal son, however, obscures the hard work of suffrage supporters that led to Burn's decisive vote as well as the continuing fierce opposition to the expansion of the franchise. The ratification campaign in the summer of 1920 was grueling, intense, and bitter. It reflected ongoing tensions surrounding equal citizenship, gender, and race.[2] As elsewhere in the nation, but perhaps even more profoundly in the South, the question of woman suffrage was intimately entwined with racial politics. These were shaped by the Civil War, Reconstruction, and its aftermath. The expansion of Black civil rights after the Civil War, guaranteed by the Fourteenth and Fifteenth Amendments to the US Constitution, and attempts to curtail those rights set the context for debates over voting rights in the southern states for decades. These tensions helped shape the complex, difficult, and divisive fight for woman suffrage in the southern states.

The ratification campaign in the summer of 1920 was grueling, intense, and bitter. It reflected ongoing tensions surrounding equal citizenship, gender, and race. As elsewhere in the nation, but perhaps even more profoundly in the South, the question of woman suffrage was intimately entwined with racial politics. These were shaped by the Civil War, Reconstruction, and its aftermath.

* * *

Southern women, like their northern and western sisters, joined women's clubs and voluntary associations during the "age of association" of the 1830s. Two, Sarah and Angelina Grimké, daughters of a South Carolina slaveholder, were among the first American women to speak publicly on behalf of both abolition and women's rights. They did so, however, after leaving the South and moving to Philadelphia. In the 1840s and 1850s, elite white women in Virginia and elsewhere participated in political campaigns. They often aligned themselves with the Whig Party, which tended to support benevolent reform measures that attracted women's support more robustly than did the Democratic Party of the era. The Whig Party even celebrated women's civic contributions.[3] But although individual women favored voting rights, very little organized support of opening the franchise to women existed in the southern states in the antebellum period.

During Reconstruction, some southern women did seek to create suffrage organizations, founding branches of the American Woman Suffrage Association (AWSA) or the National Woman Suffrage Association (NWSA). The end of the Civil War and passage of three constitutional amendments, the Thirteenth (ending slavery), Fourteenth (promising equal birthright citizenship), and Fifteenth (prohibiting racially based disenfranchisement), engendered a national conversation about civil rights, equality, and voting rights. This was a conversation that many women sought to extend to include consideration of woman suffrage. Some southern Reconstruction-era woman suffrage organizations included Black and white women.[4] But Reconstruction's end and the ascendency of overtly racist state governments bent on undoing its reforms discouraged these coalitions. By the turn of the century, southern states had created elaborate segregation and disenfranchisement measures. These included poll taxes, literacy tests, and grandfather clauses, and the Supreme Court had upheld them as constitutional. In the post-Reconstruction era in which state governments institutionalized white supremacy, to link woman suffrage with Black civil and voting rights discredited both movements. The nascent southern woman suffrage movement lost influence and visibility, even as individual women remained committed to the cause.

Organizational activity increased after the AWSA and NWSA merged in 1890 as the National American Woman Suffrage Association (NAWSA). NAWSA set a policy of founding local clubs across the nation, including in the South, and dedicated itself to recruiting southern women into its ranks. This strategy worked to an extent. Women created NAWSA clubs across the region, but they tended to be overly dependent on the leadership of an individual.

In the 1840s and 1850s, elite white women in Virginia and elsewhere participated in political campaigns. They often aligned themselves with the Whig Party, which tended to support benevolent reform measures that attracted women's support more robustly than did the Democratic Party of the era. The Whig Party even celebrated women's civic contributions.

These were often women who had lived part of their life in the Northeast, and clubs declined or collapsed after they left the organization. The lack of cultivation of grassroots support in the 1890s led to a decline in the southern suffrage movement in the following decade.[5]

Members of the Equal Suffrage League of Virginia posing near the Robert E. Lee Monument in Richmond.

* * *

After 1910, energized partially by the expansion of the national movement under the leadership of Carrie Chapman Catt and the successes of referenda in western states, the southern movement gained new strength. There were reasons specific to the region for the increase of support as well. Southern suffragists tended to be members of the new urban middle class. Their fathers and husbands, and sometimes they themselves, took part in the industrializing economy. They were in positions that linked them to a national market or to urban centers, such as in small business, education, the law, and local banking. This distinguished them from the traditional southern elite tied to the plantation economy and industries that served them—textile manufacturing, railroads, and mining. Southern suffrage supporters often had an advanced education, sometimes a college education. A few had attended northeastern women's colleges. Many worked for part of their lives in the new urban economy, often as teachers or in family businesses. As elsewhere, many of these women became involved in Progressive-Era reform. As settlement workers, clubwomen, and missionaries, they responded to the new problems created by urbanization and industrialization and exercising skills they gained through education and employment. For example, Atlanta, the archetypical New South city, grew from 9,554 people in 1860 to over 65,000 in 1890 to over 150,000 in 1910. It became a center for Black and white women's employment and social activism. It was not until after 1910 that the region produced a critical mass of "new women of the New South" as the economy industrialized and urbanized. Many of these women became interested in expanding education, abolishing child labor and the convict lease system, improving city services, and, through their support for reform, attracted to the suffrage cause.[6]

* * *

During the pivotal decade of the 1910s, southern women lent their support to woman suffrage organizations that varied widely in their political objectives and strategies. Most joined local groups associated with NAWSA such as the Equal Suffrage League of Virginia. A few affiliated themselves with Alice Paul's National Woman's Party (NWP), an organization single-mindedly focused on a national amendment. Smaller in number but influential was the uniquely southern states' rights suffrage movement. Headed by Kate Gordon of Louisiana, the southern states' rights suffragists opposed a federal amendment while pressuring state legislatures to enfranchise women—or, to be more accurate, white women. Gordon, who created the Era (or Equal Rights for All) Club in New Orleans in 1896, explicitly viewed state-level woman suffrage measures as a way to maintain white supremacy and a majority white electorate. Her visibility as head of the Era Club gained her the support of NAWSA and in 1903 the position of corresponding

Kate Gordon of New Orleans, supporter of "state's rights suffrage" and opponent of a federal amendment. Gordon viewed suffrage for white women as a way to strengthen white supremacy.

secretary of the organization. NAWSA leadership hoped that Gordon could help expand the movement in the southern states. But over time, her unyielding support of the states' rights approach alienated her from the national movement.[7]

* * *

In this racially hostile environment, Black women who sought equal civil and political rights knew that outspoken resistance to the status quo could be met by violence. Yet African American women born in the South had a profound influence on the suffrage movement, often after they left the region.

In 1913, responding to the growing support for a national amendment, Gordon formed the Southern States Woman Suffrage Conference (SSWSC). The motto of its journal, "Make the Southern States White," underlined its view of the goal of enfranchising white women. Envisioned and funded as a branch of NAWSA, Gordon's organization was increasingly at odds with the national group, and even an outright adversary. Most southern suffragists disagreed with Gordon's rejection of a national amendment and the national organization and found her attempt to defeat both counterproductive. In Louisiana, the division between SSWSC supporters and NAWSA members was acrimonious and destructive. Gordon refused to work with a NAWSA-affiliated group in 1918 to support a proposed state suffrage amendment that she favored. Though passed by the legislature, it failed ratification by the electorate. This defeat stemmed from a variety of sources, including opposition from a powerful New Orleans political machine steadfastly opposed to reform movements of all kinds. But Gordon's hostility toward other suffrage supporters weakened the movement in Louisiana. She continued to oppose a national amendment, actively campaigning against the Nineteenth Amendment, because it would enfranchise Black women. Many white southerners, like Gordon, feared that a national woman suffrage amendment would bring increased federal scrutiny of elections and enforcement of the Fourteenth and Fifteenth Amendments. Racial ideology was central to political struggles in the New South.[8]

* * *

Gordon's outspoken support of woman suffrage as a way to ensure white supremacy was not typical of those who joined groups affiliated with NAWSA or the NWP. More typical were arguments that Black women would be disenfranchised by the same measures that disenfranchised Black men. As a pamphlet from the Equal Suffrage League of Virginia asserted, "As these [state-level voting] laws restrict the negro man's vote, it stands to reason that they will also restrict the negro woman's vote." NAWSA and NWP affiliates sought to politely avoid the race question, denouncing neither Black disenfranchisement nor the overtly racist language of Gordon and her allies. White woman suffragists' lack of support for Black women's (and men's) voting rights points to their regrettable acceptance of Jim Crow in the southern states and in much of the nation.[9]

In this racially hostile environment, Black women who sought equal civil and political rights knew that outspoken resistance to the status quo could be met by violence. Yet African American women born in the South had a profound influence on the suffrage movement, often after they left the region. Ida B. Wells-Barnett, born in 1892 in Holly Springs, Mississippi, advocated for civil rights, women's rights including suffrage, and an end to lynching. She did so from her adopted home of Chicago, where she settled after her life was threatened in Memphis. In Chicago, she founded the Women's Era Club and later the Alpha Suffrage Club of Chicago, the first Black woman's club dedicated to voting rights for women. Despite the indifference or even hostility she faced from white suffrage activists, she continued to push for enfranchisement of Black women. Taking part in the significant 1913 parade in Washington, DC, sponsored by NAWSA, Wells refused to march in the back as instructed and instead joined the rest of the Illinois delegation.[10]

* * *

Some Black women advocated for suffrage while remaining in the South.[11] Mary Church Terrell, born in Memphis, Tennessee, graduated from Oberlin College

Mary Church Terrell, born in Memphis and active in Washington, DC, viewed woman suffrage as an essential component of achieving civil rights for African Americans.

and spent most of her career in Washington, DC. A writer and educator, she headed an active suffrage movement in that city and associated herself with the Republican Party.[12] In urban areas, such as Atlanta, Black female Progressives viewed suffrage for all as essential for securing civil rights.[13] Black women in Nashville supported suffrage from a variety of secular and church organizations. After Tennessee women won the right to vote in municipal elections in 1919, Black and white clubwomen of that city created a coalition designed to increase the political influence of both. Making a class- and gender-based alliance, Nashville women worked to enact educational and social service reform, as well as Black representation in municipal services. This alliance was both remarkable and unusual. Typically, white suffrage supporters avoided association with Black women and attempted to downplay the accusations of anti-suffrage activists that woman suffrage would increase Black women's political influence.

Indeed, anti-suffragists played on racial anxieties in their attempt to resist woman suffrage in the South. Georgia, the first state to vote against ratification of the Nineteenth Amendment, had a particularly visible "anti" movement.[14] In 1914, they formed the Georgia Association Opposed to Woman Suffrage (GAOWS). This was the first southern branch of the National Association Opposed to Woman Suffrage, founded in New York City in response to the growing power of the movement in the Northeast.[15] As was true for anti-suffragists elsewhere, female opponents to suffrage in the South feared that the vote would "desex" women, destroy the home, and lessen, rather than strengthen, women's power and influence.[16] As leading Georgia anti Mildred Lewis Rutherford declared in 1912, "if there is a power that is placed in any hands, it is the power that is placed in the hands of the southern woman in her home. . . . That power is great enough to direct legislative bodies—and that, too, without demanding the ballot."[17] Additionally, southern antis feared that a federal woman suffrage amendment would violate the racial order, since it would bring increased, and unwelcome, scrutiny to southern elections. Anti-suffrage propaganda often pointed to the "horrors" of Reconstruction, especially Black voting power, as a cautionary tale against extending the franchise.[18] Antis also worried that that the intimidation techniques used against Black men would not work against women. As a Virginia newspaper declared, "We have managed the men, but could we manage the women? It is a different proposition. We

> *"[I]f there is a power that is placed in any hands, it is the power that is placed in the hands of the southern woman in her home. . . . That power is great enough to direct legislative bodies— and that, too, without demanding the ballot."*
>
> —Mildred Lewis Rutherford

believe that most of the women would qualify and we further believe that they would persuade many of the men to qualify; and pay their poll taxes for them if need be."[19] Southern antis pointed to Black women's educational and employment gains by the 1890s, asserting that Black women outpaced Black men in literacy and in determination to pay their poll tax even if it they would "go hungry."[20] Antis believed that whites needed total control over voting (not just a majority of votes) by state-level restrictions to maintain political dominance.

* * *

Antis proved influential and formidable. In 1920 only Texas and Arkansas had full voting rights for (white) women. Tennessee allowed voting in presidential elections and citywide elections. A few states, including Kentucky, Mississippi, and Louisiana, allowed women to vote in some school elections. Women voted in some cities in Florida on municipal matters. Of the southern states that ratified the Nineteenth Amendment, all—Kentucky, Texas, Arkansas, and Tennessee—had some degree of state-level female enfranchisement. After the ratification of the Nineteenth Amendment, many southern women—especially Black women, but also some white women—found themselves disenfranchised by poll taxes and other measures.[21] Despite the success of the federal amendment, antidemocratic forces in state and local politics continued to limit the ability of southern women to exercise the right to vote.

* * *

At the turn of the twentieth century, as southern legislators sought to limit the franchise for African American men, many white southerners were loathe to support any expansion of voting rights. Whereas antis tended to openly advocate support for racial inequality, white suffrage supporters approached the issue in different ways. Some viewed white women's enfranchisement as a way to ensure white supremacy, others downplayed the issue. A small number formed coalitions with Black women. Southern African American women viewed woman suffrage as part the struggle for civil rights and racial equality. In the early twentieth-century South, the debate over woman suffrage was inextricably linked with contemporary views on race, Black disenfranchisement, and white supremacy.

In the early twentieth-century South, the debate over woman suffrage was inextricably linked with contemporary views on race, Black disenfranchisement, and white supremacy.

At this January 24, 1928, gathering of two hundred women at the Asociación de Reporteros in Havana, Cuba, five US National Woman's Party members joined Cuban suffragists in plans to inject women's rights into the Sixth International Conference of American States meeting in Havana. Several days later, they marched in the streets of Havana and gained a hearing at the conference, where they argued for an equal rights treaty and pushed for the creation of the Inter-American Commission of Women. Cuban feminists would use this and other inter-American organizations to connect with other Latin American feminists and to push for suffrage, granted there in 1934.

The American women's suffrage movement did not happen in a vacuum, and its influence did not stop at the US border. The push for women's rights in America and overseas was inspired in part by the French, Haitian, and American Revolutions in the eighteenth century. Later political upheavals, including the Mexican and Russian Revolutions, also had effects on the struggle for women's rights.

The first Women's Rights Convention took place in Seneca Falls, New York in 1848. It was one of the first organized efforts to demand women's equality, and was strongly connected to the global politics of the time. Indeed, the catalyst for the convention was the experiences of Elizabeth Cady Stanton and Lucretia Mott at the World Anti-Slavery Convention in London, England in 1840. Forbidden to speak at the meeting because they were women, Stanton and Mott carried

their frustrations home and organized the 1848 convention. Of the over three hundred Seneca Falls Convention attendees, one hundred women and men signed the Declaration of Sentiments. This document spelled out women's demands for equality. Mott, a Quaker minister and abolitionist, attended the convention and explicitly connected the Declaration of Sentiments to the abolition of slavery in the French West Indies, opposition to the US war with Mexico, and Native American rights. Mott associated American women's efforts to gain enfranchisement with a broader struggle for civil liberties across ethnicities and nationalities. In the following decades, American suffragists continued their fight for suffrage on the international stage. Stanton, for example,

Starting in 1915, "America First" had become a slogan used by isolationists who wanted to keep the United States out of World War I. In 1917, when this political cartoon appeared on the cover of the National Woman's Party publication, the Russian Revolution and its promise of equal rights for women became lightning rods for US suffragists. Referring to Russia in their protests became a strategy to embarrass the United States and indicated the broader, transformative goals many of them believed would come with the right to vote. Nina Allender, "America First!/Russia First Universal Suffrage,"1917.

A Strong Sweep and a Long Sweep Will Do It!

To Make the Whole World Safe for Future Generations the Women Voters of All Nations, With Their Ballots, Must Sweep Away the Traffic in Alcoholic Beverages.

The WCTU's global vision of suffrage, as well as the connections it drew between suffrage, domesticity, and temperance are illustrated in this cover of the Union Signal, the official publication of the US WCTU, March 17, 1921.

founded the International Council of Women (ICW) in 1888 to champion rights for women.

Immigrant women and women of color played pivotal roles in the women's suffrage movement. Arriving in the Unites States from all parts of the world, immigrant women brought their own ideas of what freedom and liberty entailed. Mathilde Anneke, a German immigrant, established the first women's rights journal in the United States published by a woman. Mexican-born Teresa Villarreal published the first feminist newspaper in Texas. The deplorable working conditions that many immigrant women endured also added fuel to the movement. This was especially true following the 1911 Triangle Shirtwaist Factory fire that killed 145 workers, most of whom were young, immigrant women.

Women of color were active in the American suffrage movement, yet they faced marginalization and hostility from their white counterparts. A number of white suffragist organizations adopted "imperial feminism"— the belief that white women needed to "uplift" other ethnicities at home and abroad. Women such as Ida B. Wells, Frances Ellen Watkins Harper, and Mary Church Terrell, however, continued to show up to local and national suffrage meetings and events as well as forming their own organizations. African American suffragists continued to connect global ideals of freedom with local women's rights issues, broadening their fight for greater civil liberties to include universal suffrage for men and women, anti-lynching, and education.

Read more about the international roots and legacies of the American women's suffrage movement in Katherine Marino's essay, "The International History of the US Suffrage Movement" at https://www.nps.gov/articles/the-internationalist-history-of-the-us-suffrage-movement.htm.

—Katherine Crawford-Lackey

The officers and delegates to the first convention of the Women's Christian Temperance Union (WCTU) in Skagway, Alaska, May 13-17, 1915. The Woman's Christian Temperance Union, a leading organization in calling for prohibition, also had a major impact on women's calls for suffrage rights. Members of the WCTU supported women's suffrage as they believed enfranchisement would enable them to use their voting power to enact prohibition and curtail men's alcohol use.

Commemorating Suffrage: Historic Sites and Women's Right to Vote

by Judith Wellman

Women have always been leaders in the movement for historic preservation. Until the late twentieth century, however, very few sites relating to women's history—and even fewer relating to woman suffrage—were formally identified or preserved. Beginning in the mid-nineteenth century, when Ann Pamela Cunningham and the Mount Vernon Ladies' Association rescued George Washington's home from decay, historic preservationists commemorated buildings associated with famous European American politicians and generals. Historic preservation seemed inconsequential to most women's rights advocates. When Cunningham tried to enlist suffrage leader Elizabeth Cady Stanton as a lady manager of the association, Stanton urged that women work on women's rights rather than historic house preservation: "Every energy of my body and soul is pledged to a higher and holier work than building monuments. . . . What mightier monument can we raise to the memory of Washington than to complete the pure temple of liberty."[1] Stanton did not foresee that her own house in Seneca Falls, New York, would one day be preserved as part of the first national park devoted to the telling of the story of women's struggle to win the vote.

Until the late twentieth century, with few exceptions, historic preservation reinforced a historical narrative that excluded most women and people of color. That began to change in the 1960s, when the rise of social history coincided with new trends in historic preservation. Inspired by civil rights and feminist movements and the growing field of heritage tourism, historians and preservationists began to emphasize the importance of historic sites that reflected the lived experience of Americans of all races, classes, and genders. Many states, communities, and public and nonprofit agencies began to highlight women's history sites. A handful of these dealt with woman suffrage.[2] Almost all of these related to the organized movement from 1848 to 1920, ignoring both suffrage efforts before 1848 and attempts to implement suffrage, especially for people of color, after 1920. Many sites recognized primarily for

Until the late twentieth century, with few exceptions, historic preservation reinforced a historical narrative that excluded most women and people of color. That began to change in the 1960s, when the rise of social history coincided with new trends in historic preservation.

their association with other historical events, however, also began to incorporate the story of woman suffrage, recognizing a more inclusive definition of suffrage work.

* * *

Around the turn of the twentieth century, three sites—one of them related directly to woman suffrage—challenged the primary historic preservation emphasis on military sites and great white men. In 1901, the Christian Science Church purchased the Mary Baker Eddy house in Lynn, Massachusetts, to preserve it as the home of the founder of a worldwide religion. In 1912, the United Women's Club of Concord, Massachusetts, opened Orchard House, the home of Louisa May Alcott, author of *Little Women*, to the public.[3] The third exception, and the first related directly to woman suffrage, was the preservation of Frederick Douglass's home at Cedar Hill in Washington, DC.

Douglass's home at Cedar Hill was saved primarily by the work of women, including Helen Pitts Douglass, Douglass's second wife. Beginning in 1903, Archibald Grimké, Booker T. Washington, and Mary B. Talbert, president of the National Association of Colored Women's Clubs, worked to raise money to pay off the mortgage, restore the home, and open it to the public. Madam C. J. Walker, America's first woman millionaire, gave generously to this effort.[4]

Frederick Douglass National Historic Site, Cedar Hill, Washington, DC.

By the 1920s, women became leaders in a new effort to preserve historic neighborhoods and communities, including buildings both grand and modest. Susan Pringle Frost was a pathbreaker. In 1920, she founded what became the Preservation Society of Charleston, the oldest locally based preservation organization in the United States. Like many preservationists, Frost was also an advocate of woman suffrage. But she did not translate her political interests into saving historic sites relating to suffrage.[5] The first major historic site preserved primarily for its relationship to woman suffrage was the Susan B. Anthony home at 17 Madison Street in Rochester, New York. Led by Martha Taylor Howard, the house opened in 1945 as a memorial to Anthony and the suffrage movement.[6]

By and large, however, in the first two-thirds of the twentieth century historic preservation ignored women. Even statues of women were rare. The Smithsonian Institution identified 5,575 outdoor sculptures of American historical figures. Only 200 of these, less than 4 percent, depicted women. Adelaide Johnson's statue of Stanton, Anthony, and Lucretia Mott, created in 1920 for the National Woman's Party, was immediately relegated to the basement of the US Capitol. It only returned to the Rotunda in 1997. New York City's Central Park erected a statue of Mother Goose in 1938, one of Alice in Wonderland in 1959, and a third of Juliet (and Romeo) in 1977, alongside those of twenty-two real men. A proposed statue of Stanton, Anthony, and Sojourner Truth would represent the first commemoration of real women in Central Park.

In the late twentieth century, neglect of historic sites relating to women began to change. In 1960, Congress created the National Historic Landmarks program to mark exceptionally important buildings. In 1966, it passed a new historic preservation act, establishing both the National Register of Historic Places and State Historic Preservation Offices in every state.[7] The new National Register's criteria corresponded with the explosion of interest in social history and women's history. This was inspired by movements for civil rights and women's rights. History "from the bottom up" emphasized issues of gender, race, and class, highlighting the experience of all Americans. A new interest in women's history emerged as part of an emphasis on the built environment and urban landscapes that included ordinary Americans.[8]

Reflecting this new scholarship, preservationists began to explore the importance of historic sites relating to women. Federal agencies helped energize this movement. The National Historic Landmarks

program led the way with a survey authorized in 1975 of sites relating to minority groups. At the same time, Page Putnam Miller directed the Women's History Landmark Project. It was cosponsored by the National Park Service (NPS), the Organization of American Historians, and the National Coordinating Committee for the Promotion of History. In 1992, Miller published results of that study, *Reclaiming Our Past: Landmarks of Women's History.* In 1994, the NPS adopted a new thematic framework, published in 1996 as *History in the National Park Service: Themes and Concepts,* incorporating many ideas from the new social history.[9] The NPS also sponsored several conferences on women and historic preservation. In 2003, selections from these conferences appeared in Gail Lee Dubrow and Jennifer B. Goodman, eds., *Restoring Women's History through Historic Preservation.*[10]

With assistance from the National Park Service, forty representatives of historic sites and organizations formed the National Collaborative for Women's History Sites to promote "the preservation and interpretation of sites and locales that bear witness to women's participation in American life."

These conferences acted as an incubator for a new organization. With assistance from the National Park Service, forty representatives of historic sites and organizations formed the National Collaborative for Women's History Sites to promote "the preservation and interpretation of sites and locales that bear witness to women's participation in American life." Heather Huyck, NPS historian and a member of the original steering committee, noted, "leaving women out of the story is as serious a distortion of our history as trying to tell the history of the Civil War without talking about Black history."[11] Preservation efforts focused on (1) publicizing existing women's history sites, (2) identifying and preserving previously unmarked historic sites relating to women, and (3) interpreting women's history at traditionally male-dominated sites. Though not focused on woman suffrage sites per se, these goals provided a context for suffrage as one theme among many.

In 1994, Lynn Sherr and Jurate Kazickas published *Susan B. Anthony Slept Here: A Guide to American Women's Landmarks,* a revision of their *American Woman's*

Home of Alice Paul, Paulsdale,
Mt. Laurel, New Jersey.

Gazetteer (1976), to publicize existing women's history
sites. Several states and cities developed women's history
trails. Many states also developed women's biographical
collections and halls of fame. These supplemented the
National Women's Hall of Fame, organized in Seneca Falls,
New York in 1969. In 1998, spurred by the commemoration
of the 150th anniversary of the first women's rights convention in Seneca Falls, the National Register initiated a travel
guide. *Places Where Women Made History* highlighted
seventy-five sites in New York and Massachusetts. In 2009,
Congress authorized the Votes for Women History Trail
Route. Introduced by Congresswoman Louise Slaughter,
the trail never received funding.[12]

At the same time, beginning in the 1990s, several
public and nonprofit groups acquired homes of major
suffrage leaders. The Alice Paul Institute purchased
the Alice Paul home in 1990, to commemorate Paul's
work as founder of the National Woman's Party.
The National Nineteenth Amendment Society purchased Carrie Chapman Catt's home in Iowa in 1991
to interpret the early life of Catt. She had served as

president of the National American Woman Suffrage Association. In 1999, a nonprofit group acquired the Susan B. Anthony birthplace in Adams, Massachusetts, after years of efforts to preserve the homestead that began in 1910. The Matilda Joslyn Gage Foundation organized in 2000 to preserve and interpret the Gage home as a center of suffrage, the Underground Railroad, Native American rights, and liberal religion in Fayetteville, New York. In 2001, the Buffalo Niagara Freedom Station Coalition interpreted the Michigan Street Baptist Church as a major site of African American activism, including woman suffrage. In 2006, New York State acquired the home where Susan B. Anthony lived in the 1830s in Battenkill, New York. It still awaits restoration.[13]

The National Historic Landmarks program also promoted sites relating to major woman suffrage leaders. In 1965, the homes of both Elizabeth Cady Stanton in Seneca Falls and Susan B. Anthony in Rochester, New York, became National Historic Landmarks. More sites followed: Harriet Tubman in Auburn, New York (1974 and 2001), Madam C. J. Walker in Irvington, New York (1976), Mary Ann Shadd Cary in Washington, DC (1976), Alice Paul in Mount Laurel, New Jersey (1991), Gerrit Smith in Peterboro, New York (2001),

Top: Carrie Chapman Catt Girlhood Home, Charles City, Iowa.

Left: Michigan Street Baptist Church, Mary Talbert's church, Buffalo, New York.

Carrie Chapman Catt in Charles City, Iowa, and New Castle, New York, and Abigail Scott Duniway in Portland, Oregon. In 2012, the NPS held a conference at the Belmont-Paul House in Washington, DC. Cosponsored with the National Collaborative for Women's History Sites, attendees considered how women's stories could best be included as National Historic Landmarks. As a result of that effort, seven more women's history sites were added to the National Historic Landmarks program.[14]

By 2000, the National Park Service had opened seven parks related specifically to women. In 1980, Women's Rights National Historical Park commemorated the first women's rights convention, held in July 1848 in Seneca Falls, New York. By 2018, the National Park Service had added three more sites dealing specifically with women. One, the Belmont-Paul Women's Equality National Monument (formerly the Sewall-Belmont House), headquarters for the National Woman's Party, related specifically to suffrage. It was designated a National Monument in 2016.[15]

Despite these efforts, the number of historic sites related specifically to women remained only a small proportion of the whole. The number of sites that dealt with suffrage was even smaller. The ten national parks that dealt directly with women, for example, made up 20 percent of the fifty-one national historical parks in the National Park Service. Only two of these—Women's Rights National Historical Park and the Belmont-Paul Women's Equality National Monument—dealt directly with woman suffrage. Of the seven women's history sites listed as National Historic Landmarks since 2011, only two—the homes of Frances Perkins and Marjory Stoneman Douglas—were linked to suffragists.[16] The pattern was repeated at the state level. In New York State, for example, only one state park, Sonnenberg Gardens, related directly to a woman. None dealt specifically with woman suffrage. The National Register's "Places Where Women Made History" listed thirty-five sites in New York, eight of which related to suffrage. Five of these were part of Women's Rights National Historical Park in Seneca Falls.[17]

In the late twentieth century, women's historians and historic preservationists, including the National Park Service and the National Collaborative for Women's History Sites, also pushed for the interpretation of women at historic sites typically associated with men. The NPS published *Exploring a Common Past: Researching and Interpreting Women's History for Historic Sites* in 1996; Polly Welts Kaufman and

In the late twentieth century, women's historians and historic preservationists, including the National Park Service and the National Collaborative for Women's History Sites, also pushed for the interpretation of women at historic sites typically associated with men.

Facing page: Wesleyan Chapel, site of the first women's rights convention, 1848, Seneca Falls, New York.

Katharine T. Corbett edited *Her Past around Us: Interpreting Sites for Women's History* in 2003; and the National Collaborative for Women's History Sites published a number of reports in the early 2000s. This emphasis has had a powerful effect. Today, historic site interpreters routinely include references to women at sites once considered the focus only of male history. These include battlefields, homes of politicians, churches, factories, farms, plantations, and Native American sites.[18]

Interpreting women's history at historic sites relating primarily to men offers a model for interpreting woman suffrage at a wide variety of historic sites preserved for unrelated reasons. Helen Keller, for example (whose home in Tuscumbia, Alabama, is listed as a National Historic Landmark), spoke out for woman suffrage as well as for socialism, workers' rights, and blind and deaf people. Frances Perkins, best known for her work as secretary of labor under Franklin Delano Roosevelt, grew up in a suffrage family and gave suffrage speeches herself. Perkins's house in Washington, DC, became a National Historic Landmark in 1991, and her family home in Newcastle, Maine, was listed in 2014. Marjory Stoneman Douglas is best known for her work as the author of *The Everglades: River of Grass* (1947), but she also championed racial justice, women's rights, and woman suffrage, giving a suffrage speech before the Florida house of representatives in 1916. Her home in Coconut Grove, Florida, was listed as a National Historic Landmark in 2015.[19]

And then there is Frederick Douglass. Although the National Park Service includes Douglass's work for women's rights in its interpretation of Cedar Hill, suffrage historians have not highlighted Douglass's home as a suffrage site. They should. Douglass consistently supported suffrage for women as well as African Americans, beginning at Seneca Falls in 1848. "We know of no truth more easily made appreciable to human thought than the right of woman to vote, or in other words, to have a voice in the Government under which she lives and to which she owes allegiance," he asserted in 1870. He never deviated from that position and found, as he said in 1888, "a little nobility in the act" of supporting women's rights.[20]

Renewed interest in the suffrage movement, centered around the one hundredth anniversary of the Nineteenth Amendment, offers an opportunity to add to the list of known suffrage sites.

* * *

Renewed interest in the suffrage movement, centered around the one hundredth anniversary of the Nineteenth Amendment, offers an opportunity to add to the list of known suffrage sites. The woman suffrage movement began much earlier than 1848 and lasted far beyond 1920, and it extended to US territories such as Puerto Rico. Margaret Brent asked for a vote in the Maryland colonial assembly in 1648. After 1920, attempts to implement suffrage for both men and women often resulted in violent confrontations, especially for African Americans in the South. Not until 1935 did woman suffrage become legal for all Puerto Rican women. It took a court case initiated by an Isleta Indian and US veteran before New Mexico recognized voting rights for Native American in 1948. In 1962, Utah was the last state to enfranchise Native Americans. Asian American immigrants were routinely denied citizenship until 1952. The Voting Rights Act of 1965 helped protect suffrage everywhere, but in *Shelby v. Holder* (2013), the Supreme Court gutted the Voting Rights Act. [21]

New scholarly work provides the basis for identifying suffrage sites defined by wide chronological, geographic, and cultural/ethnic boundaries. Working with local historians and interested citizens, for example, the William G. Pomeroy Foundation by 2018 had erected thirty-three markers at suffrage sites across New York. By the fall of 2019, the National Votes for Women Trail, developed by the National Collaborative for Women's History Sites, had located more than one thousand woman suffrage sites in almost forty states. Working with the Pomeroy Foundation, the National Votes for Women Trail will erect 250 suffrage markers across the nation by 2020. [22] In 2016 Nashville, Tennessee commemorated five women who helped promote Tennessee's ratification of the Nineteenth Amendment. By 2020 a statue of suffragist Ida B. Wells will be erected in Chicago. Another is planned for Fairfax County, Virginia, to honor suffragists imprisoned in Occoquan Prison for picketing the White House. And, a statue of Susan B. Anthony, Elizabeth Cady Stanton, and Sojourner Truth will become the first monument erected to real women in Central Park in New York City. [23]

Historic sites related to women's suffrage from the earliest years to the present offer inspiration from the past and guideposts toward the future. Celebrating passage of the Nineteenth Amendment on August 26, 1920 Carrie Chapman Catt declared, "Women have suffered agony of soul which you can never comprehend, that you and your daughters might inherit political freedom. That vote has been costly. Prize it!"[24] Historic sites related to woman suffrage remind us to prize that vote—for women and for all citizens of our democracy.

Historic sites related to women's suffrage from the earliest years to the present offer inspiration from the past and guideposts toward the future.

Beyond 1920: The Legacies of Woman Suffrage

by Liette Gidlow

On a sweltering August afternoon in 1920, the struggle of generations to enfranchise women on the same terms as men seemed to come to a triumphant end. Seventy-two years earlier, Elizabeth Cady Stanton, Lucretia Mott, and their intrepid peers had shocked polite society by demanding the right to vote and a raft of other rights for women. Now, every signer of their bold "Declaration of Sentiments," save one, was dead. Woman suffragists had persisted through countless trials and humiliations to get to this moment. Not only had they spoken out, organized, petitioned, traveled, marched, and raised funds; some also had endured assault, jail, and starvation to advance the cause. When the Tennessee legislature voted to ratify the Nineteenth Amendment, that right was finally won.

The Nineteenth Amendment officially eliminated sex as a barrier to voting throughout the United States. It expanded voting rights to more people than any other single measure in American history. And yet, the legacy of the Nineteenth Amendment, in the short term and over the next century, turned out to be complicated. It advanced equality between the sexes but left intersecting inequalities of class, race, and ethnicity intact. It stimulated important policy changes but left many reform goals unachieved. It helped women, above all white women, find new footings in government agencies, political parties, and elected offices—and, in time, even run for president. And yet, it left most outside the halls of power. Hardly the end of the struggle for diverse women's equality, the Nineteenth Amendment became a crucial step, but only a step, in the continuing quest for more representative democracy.

Hardly the end of the struggle for diverse women's equality, the Nineteenth Amendment became a crucial step, but only a step, in the continuing quest for more representative democracy.

* * *

Once ratification had been achieved, neither the general public nor professional politicians knew quite what to expect when election season arrived in fall 1920. Both suffragists and "Antis" had promised big changes if the Nineteenth Amendment became law. Any prediction was bound to be exaggerated, if only because women in fifteen states already enjoyed full suffrage by state action before the federal amendment had passed.[1] Suffragists had promised that women voters would clean up politics and enact a sweeping agenda of Progressive reforms. Antis grew concerned that the dirty business of politics would compromise women's moral standing. They worried that women who took part in public affairs might abandon their traditional responsibilities at home.[2] And how would polling places handle the influx of new voters? Election officials in Jersey City, New Jersey, took no chances. They ordered containers "the size of flour barrels" to hold all the votes.[3] Nor was it clear how new women voters would change the balance of political power. Republicans prognosticated that new women voters would choose the party of Lincoln to express their "gratitude for passage of [the] suffrage amendment."[4] Democrats countered that new women voters would choose them instead, and perhaps even "rescue the League of Nations" from political death.[5] Perhaps women would reject both major parties and organize into a party of their own, maximizing their power by voting as a bloc. New York City's political bosses at Tammany Hall worried that "wild women" voters might send the "great machine wobbling" if they elected to vote independently rather than toe the party line.[6] Still others predicted that woman suffrage would make no difference at all. They believed that women—intimidated by the complexities of voting or uninterested in politics altogether—would simply stay home.

When the first election returns after ratification were tallied, the impact of new women voters on the results defied simple description. Overall, fewer women voted than men, with female turnout averaging two-thirds the rate of men. The big picture, however, obscured a great deal of variation at the state and local levels. Women's turnout varied from a high of 57 percent in Kentucky to a low of 6 percent in Virginia, and the gap in turnout between the sexes ranged from 28 percent in Missouri and Kentucky to 40 percent in Connecticut. Everywhere the particular political and legal context influenced the turnout rate. For all voters, turnout tended to be higher in states with competitive races or in localities with well-organized parties. In areas with lopsided contests or layers of voting restrictions, turnout generally lagged.[7]

Apart from the election tallies, full suffrage expanded the opportunities for women to seek elected office and shape public policy. Many women had run for political office before the Nineteenth Amendment—3,701 since the Civil War, by some scholars' count, some of them in places in which women could not yet vote. Still, full enfranchisement spurred a number of female firsts.[8] In

Apart from the election tallies, full suffrage expanded the opportunities for women to seek elected office and shape public policy.

Yoncalla, Oregon, temperance-minded voters replaced the entire city council with women backed by the Woman's Christian Temperance Union ("Sex Uprising in Yoncalla," blared the *New York Times*).[9] At least twenty-two women between 1920 and 1923 were elected mayor in small towns including Langley, Washington; Salina, Utah; Red Cloud, Nebraska; Goodhue, Minnesota; Fairport, Ohio; and Duluth, Georgia. Iowa City, home to more than ten thousand residents, became the biggest city yet to elect a female mayor when it voted in Emma Harvat in 1923.[10] Bertha Landes became the first female big-city mayor when, in 1926, she filled in as acting mayor of Seattle for a stretch. Two years later, Seattleites elected her to her own term.[11]

Women enjoyed new success in state government elections as well. In 1920 teacher Eva Hamilton became the first woman elected to the Michigan Senate.[12] Four years later, Cora Belle Reynolds Anderson won election to the Michigan house, the first Native American woman in the nation to win a state legislative seat.[13] New Mexico elected the first woman to a high-ranking statewide office in 1923 when it elected Soledad Chacon as secretary of state. At least five other states—South Dakota, Texas, Kentucky, New York, and Delaware—elected women to the same office in the 1920s. Indiana elected the first female state treasurer, Grace B. Urbahns, in 1926.[14]

Suffragist Minnie Fisher Cunningham, pictured, ran for the US Senate in Texas in 1927. She lost, but later went to work for President Franklin Roosevelt's New Deal.

At the federal level, too, women ran stand-out races; occasionally they even won. Minnie Fisher Cunningham led Texas's successful campaign for woman suffrage in primary elections in 1918. In 1927, the future New Dealer ran for the US Senate. She lost the primary, but threw her support to another candidate who squeaked out a win against the incumbent Democrat, an official who was in the pocket of the Ku Klux Klan.[15] In 1928, in a remarkable development, the daughters of two of the nation's most powerful men of the previous generation—men who worked on opposing sides in the storied presidential race of 1896—both won election to the US House of Representatives. Ruth Hanna McCormick, the daughter of William McKinley's campaign manager, Marc Hanna, won election from Illinois as a Republican. She advocated for Prohibition, farmers' interests, and isolationism during her single term of service. Ruth Bryan Owen, daughter of "Cross of Gold" orator William Jennings Bryan, won election from Florida as a Democrat. She earned praise for her advocacy of child welfare as well as Florida's agricultural interests. Owen's father, the three-time Democratic nominee (and three-time loser) for the presidency, might have smiled from beyond the grave at his daughter's accomplishment. Owen joked about her win: "There! I am the first Bryan who ran for anything and got it!"[16]

Of course, women had participated in political parties well before enfranchisement. In 1920, however, both the Republican and Democratic organizations created new positions for women.

Political parties also found new places for women with interests in politics. Of course, women had participated in political parties well before enfranchisement. In 1920, however, both the Republican and Democratic organizations created new positions for women. They showcased women at their national conventions; they placed women on party committees; and they created new Women's Divisions for the purpose of integrating new women voters into the party.[17] A few exceptional women such as Harriet Taylor Upton, Emily Newell Blair, and Eleanor Roosevelt exerted unusual influence in political parties. Political advertising expert Belle Moskowitz became Al Smith's closest political advisor. She helped him win the governorship of New York and guided his 1928 presidential bid.[18]

Empowered by full suffrage, women likewise made greater inroads into the executive branch. In the summer of 1920, President Woodrow Wilson established a new Women's Bureau in the US Department of Labor. He appointed union organizer Mary Anderson to lead it. Anderson held that leadership post through Republican and Democratic administrations until 1944, building the agency into a powerful advocate for female workers.[19]

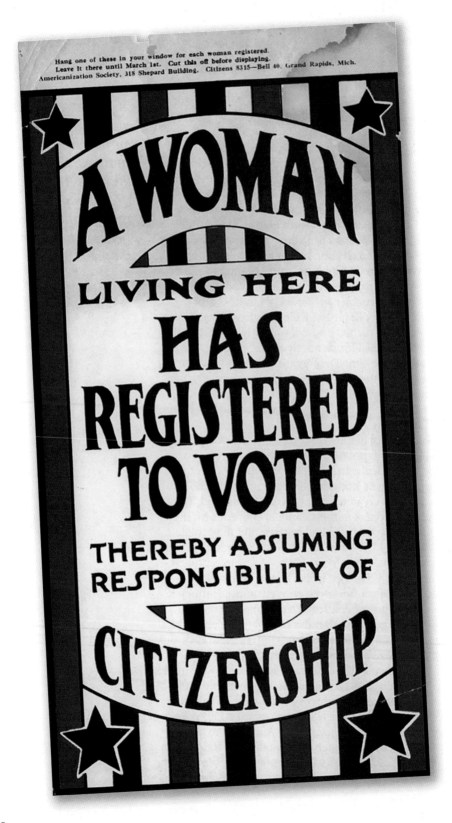

Newly enfranchised women also left their mark on public policy. After ratification, suffrage leaders forged an alliance to bring their collective political muscle to bear on the legislative process. Soon twenty organizations, including the League of Women Voters, the General Federation of Women's Clubs, the National Consumers' League, the National Women's Trade Union League, and the Woman's Christian Temperance Union, had banded together to form the Women's Joint Congressional Committee (WJCC).[20] Claiming to represent a combined membership of twenty million women, the WJCC advanced a legislative agenda that put women and children first.[21] The WJCC's efforts produced real legislative gains. The first of these, in 1921, was the Sheppard-Towner Maternity and Infancy Act. Sheppard-Towner addressed the shocking rates of infant mortality uncovered in studies by Julia Lathrop and the Children's Bureau. It provided about $1 million per year to states to fund maternal and child health clinics.[22] The Children's Bureau administered Sheppard-Towner, adding a new division to do so, thereby expanding women's foothold in the executive branch. Sheppard-Towner created a model for federal/state partnerships that the architects of the New Deal would adopt in the next decade to address the deprivations of the Depression.[23]

Women's lobbyists also succeeded in 1922 in winning congressional passage of the Cable Act. The Cable Act provided a path back to the voting booth for women who had lost their US citizenship by marrying a foreign national after 1907.[24] Women activists enjoyed additional legislative successes at the state and local level. At the federal level, they tried, without success, to win reforms on other important issues. These included the international peace movement, child labor, and lynching.

* * *

In these ways the Nineteenth Amendment expanded opportunities for women to participate in governance and changed the trajectory of social welfare policy. And yet, both suffragists and Antis had promised that ratification would do so much more. Where was the Progressive juggernaut that would solve the nation's vast social problems? Where was the chaos caused by voting women abandoning their family responsibilities? Where, in short, was the dramatic change, for good or ill, that both supporters and opponents had promised?

If full suffrage produced less change than suffragists had hoped and Antis had feared, perhaps that was partly because women did not vote as a bloc. Indeed,

Facing page: Get-Out-the-Vote activists used advertising and education campaigns to boost women's flagging turnout in the early 1920s. In Grand Rapids, Michigan, local advocates asked women to demonstrate that they had registered to vote by displaying window posters like this one. These signs resembled window posters used in the recent world war to recognize women's contributions to the war effort.

sometimes women did not vote at all. Establishment politicians soon learned that, for the most part, they did not need to worry about women voting because there was no such thing as "the women's vote." They meant that ballots cast by women increased the total but rarely changed the outcome. And, local variations aside, the overall turnout numbers for women voters were indisputably lower than men's. This fact appalled former suffragists and seemed to validate the Antis' claims that women never wanted the vote in the first place. (A Minnesota suffragist put it plaintively: "What, oh what, is Suffrage if you women will not vote?"[25]) Determined that woman suffrage would not be proved a flop, in 1924 the League of Women Voters began massive campaigns of advertising and education to "Get Out the Vote." This program, by the end of the decade, would evolve into the organization's main mission.[26]

Critics blamed nonvoting women for shirking their civic duty. One could fairly ask, however, just which women were enfranchised by the Nineteenth Amendment. States retained the ability to set conditions on access to the ballot. Bowing to party interests or racial or class bias, many states kept other barriers to voting, for men and women alike, intact or raised them higher still. By the end of the 1920s voters in forty-six states had to contend with complicated registration requirements. Residency requirements were likewise common. At the extreme, Rhode Island required citizens to live not just in the state, but in the locality, for two years before they were eligible to vote. Southern states, plus twelve more states outside the South, required literacy or educational tests.[27] These barriers may have proved more difficult for novice women voters to navigate than for men with voting experience.[28] Poll taxes certainly burdened women disproportionately. In many families the male head of household controlled the family finances, and not every husband or father was able or willing to pay the poll tax on behalf of his wife or daughter.[29]

Women's citizenship status, often complicated by their marital status, confounded access to the ballot further still. Thirty-one states had once permitted immigrants who had started the lengthy naturalization process to vote, but by the early 1920s, every state had abandoned the practice of "alien suffrage."[30] Women from some immigrant communities, especially Italians and Cubans, were far less likely to naturalize than men of the same background. Immigrants from Asia, whether male or female, could not become citizens at

Determined that woman suffrage would not be proved a flop, in 1924 the League of Women Voters began massive campaigns of advertising and education to "Get Out the Vote." This program, by the end of the decade, would evolve into the organization's main mission.

all.[31] Remarkably, the ranks of noncitizens included even some US-born women, for American women who had married a foreign national after 1907 lost their American citizenship. Unless they naturalized—and many did not pursue that lengthy legal process—they could not vote. Many Native Americans, including women, also lacked US citizenship, at least until Congress passed the Indian Citizenship Act of 1924. Even after that many indigenous people effectively rejected the US citizenship they had never asked for, preferring to be identified with their tribal communities instead. Some states continued to bar Native Americans from the ballot. In 1962, Utah was the last state to extend them the franchise.[32] None of these barriers to voting violated the Nineteenth Amendment. They all, however, made voting more difficult, and some of them made voting particularly difficult for women.

Perhaps no community was subjected to more extensive disfranchisement efforts than Black women in the Jim Crow South. Interest in voting by southern African Americans surged in the fall of 1920. Not only did many Black women seek to use their new right, but many Black men, honorably discharged from service in

African American women in the Jim Crow South were often denied the right to vote, but these nine women, all faculty members at the Virginia Normal and Collegiate Institute, succeeded in registering in the fall of 1920.

The Democratic and Republican Parties had welcomed women with great fanfare in 1920, but the Women's Divisions into which they were shunted lacked real power.

the Great War or wishing to accompany female family members, seized the moment to try to return to the polls themselves after decades of disfranchisement. In some locations, Black women succeeded in registering and voting. Those successes, even though few in number, inspired fresh efforts to suppress Black voters. Elsewhere, they were blocked by fraud, intimidation, or violence.[33] And when disfranchised black women asked the League of Women Voters and the National Woman's Party (NWP) to help, the main organizations of former suffragists turned them down. NWP head Alice Paul insisted in 1921 that Black women's disfranchisement was a "race issue," not a "woman's issue." It was therefore, she believed, no business of the NWP.[34] The failure of white suffragists at that moment to address the disfranchisement of southern Black women reverberated for decades to come. It undercut efforts of women of both races to make progress on issues of shared concern.

The impact of women's votes was also limited because the coalition that had supported suffrage splintered under the pressures of the troubled postwar political climate and competing political interests. Amid national tensions fueled by widespread labor unrest, bloody race riots, anti-immigrant animus, and anarchist violence, conservative women organized in the Daughters of the American Revolution and the Women's Auxiliary of the American Legion. They accused many Progressive women of harboring Communist sympathies.[35] Their red-baiting tactics soon brought the Sheppard-Towner Act to an end. Opposed from the beginning by organized medicine, the American Medical Association attacked it as an "imported socialistic scheme" and got Congress to defund it by 1929.[36] Progressive suffragists also divided among themselves, above all over the possibility of an equal rights amendment. Alice Paul insisted that a blanket amendment to ensure sex equality in broad areas of life must be the next item on women's agenda. Advocates for working women, however, were bitterly opposed. They had labored for decades to secure wages and hours protections and could not risk the possibility that an equal rights amendment would undo their hard-won gains.[37]

Nor did women find that full suffrage necessarily gave them greater access to the levers of power. The Democratic and Republican Parties had welcomed women with great fanfare in 1920, but the Women's Divisions into which they were shunted lacked real power. The same was frequently true at the state level. A female member of the New Jersey Republican

State Committee in 1924 noted ruefully that the state committee on which she sat met rarely and passed "a few resolutions of no importance. . . . Then the men met privately and transacted the real business."[38] In the executive branch in the 1920s women found that they exercised considerable power in select agencies, above all the Children's Bureau and Women's Bureau. And yet, they had few opportunities to influence policy outside this narrow "female dominion."[39]

* * *

The Nineteenth Amendment did not fulfill all its supporters' hopes, but it was no failure. It brought the nation closer to universal suffrage and made the injustice of ongoing disfranchisement even less defensible. It expanded opportunities for women to govern and changed the direction of public policy. It accorded women the status of decision makers in the public sphere and recognized that they had the authority to help make decisions that others—men—would have to abide. If these changes fell short of expectations, perhaps that was because expectations had been so great. Suffragist Maud Wood Park, the first leader of the League of Women Voters, remarked that it was hardly reasonable to expect women voters "over-night to straighten out tangles over which generations of men had worked in vain."[40]

Despite its limitations, the Nineteenth Amendment over the next century helped women assume a role in public affairs that would be hard to imagine without it. Women gradually closed the turnout gap between the sexes. In every presidential year since 1984, they have exceeded men in voter turnout. In 2016 the Democrats nominated Hillary Clinton to run for president, the first major party to nominate a woman as its standard-bearer. In 2019 women occupied 9 governorships, 24 seats in the US Senate, and 102 seats in the US House of Representatives. A century after ratification, it is clear that though the Nineteenth Amendment did not perfect American democracy, it advanced gender equality in important ways.

A century after ratification, it is clear that though the Nineteenth Amendment did not perfect American democracy, it advanced gender equality in important ways.

Related Sites

Women's Rights National Historical Park

Women's Rights National Historical Park

This park is located in Seneca Falls, New York. It preserves the stories of the women who led the early movement for women's suffrage (the right to vote). Women including Lucretia Mott and Elizabeth Cady Stanton organized the first Woman's Rights Convention in 1848. They held it in Seneca Falls. Attendees, including Frederick Douglass, signed a Declaration of Sentiments at the convention. This document demanded equal rights and treatment for women.

Belmont-Paul Women's Equality National Monument

Belmont-Paul Women's Equality National Monument

This National Monument is located on Capitol Hill in Washington, DC. It has served as the headquarters of the National Woman's Party (NWP) for almost a century. Co-founded by Alice Paul, the NWP used creative tactics to fight for an amendment to the Constitution that would enfranchise women. Their tactics included a months-long picket of the White House. During World War I, suffrage picketers were arrested, sent to prison, and force-fed during hunger strikes. After the ratification of the Nineteenth Amendment, the NWP moved into this building to continue the fight for social, political, and economic equality for women.

Acadia National Park

This National Park is located in Bar Harbor, Maine on the rocky headlands of the Atlantic coastline. Eliza Homans was the first person to donate land for the preservation of the park. Originally from out of state, Homans spent many summers in northern Maine. She donated approximately 140 acres of land to conserve the natural scenery.

Acadia National Park

Clara Barton National Historic Site

Clara Barton National Historic Site

Visitors to this National Historic Site in Glen Echo, Maryland, explore the home of the "Angel of the Battlefield." Clara Barton was not trained as a nurse. But when she saw that wounded men during the Civil War lacked proper care, she jumped in to help. She faced great personal danger traveling to the front lines to bring supplies, organize field hospitals and ambulance support, and provide comfort and medical assistance. After the war, she coordinated the search for missing soldiers and founded the American Red Cross.

Denali National Park and Preserve

Alaska is home to Denali National Park and Preserve. It encompasses six million acres of wild land. Denali is the tallest peak in North America, and many people, including Barbara Washburn, have hiked to the top. She was part of an expeditionary team that filmed and mapped the mountain. On June 6th, 1947, she became the first white woman to climb to the summit of Denali.

Denali National Park and Preserve

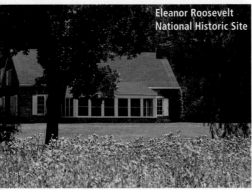

Eleanor Roosevelt National Historic Site

Eleanor Roosevelt National Historic Site

This National Historic Site is in Hyde Park, New York. It includes Val Kill, Eleanor Roosevelt's home following the death of her husband, President Franklin D. Roosevelt. Eleanor served as First Lady and influential adviser to her husband. She was also an important political leader in her own right. She lived at Val Kill where she frequently visited with her friends Marion Dickson, Nancy Cook, and Caroline O'Day. Together they established Val-Kill Industries on the property. It provided work for and supplemented the income of farming families.

Everglades National Park

This National Park is located at the southern tip of Florida. It is home to manatees, crocodiles, and many other endangered species. Marjory Stoneman Douglas, an outspoken proponent of women's suffrage, was also a tireless advocate for preserving the Everglades. In 1947, Stoneman published her book, *The Everglades: River of Grass*. It called attention to the importance of preserving this unique landscape.

Everglades National Park

Gateway Arch National Park

Known as the "gateway to the west," this National Park is located in St. Louis, Missouri. It tells the story of Americans moving west and settling lands once inhabited only by Native Americans. The park is home to the city's Old Courthouse where the Virginia Minor case was decided. A member of the National Woman Suffrage Association, Minor tried to register to vote in the 1872 presidential election. She argued that under the 14th Amendment, she was a citizen of the United States and thus entitled to vote. Her case

Gateway Arch National Park

Glacier National Park

Grand Teton National Park

went all the way to the US Supreme Court. While she ultimately lost, she brought national attention to the fight for women's suffrage.

Glacier National Park

Located in northern Montana, this National Park encompasses rugged mountains and pristine lakes. One person who chronicled her experience in the park is Mary Roberts Rinehart. A noted American author, Reinhart traveled on horseback over three hundred miles of rugged terrain. She described her travels in her book *Through Glacier Park*, published in 1916.

Grand Teton National Park

This National Park is located in northwest Wyoming. It is known for its rugged alpine terrain and extraordinary wildlife. Adventurous souls like Geraldine Lucas homesteaded near the Teton Range. After retiring from teaching, Lucas relocated to Wyoming on her own, and built a cabin near Jenny Lake. At the age of 58, she became the second white woman to climb to the top of the Grand Teton. While the National Park was being formed, Lucas refused to sell her land, even for much more than it was worth. After her death, her son sold the land and it eventually became part of Grand Teton National Park.

Great Smoky Mountains National Park

Great Smoky Mountains straddles the border of Tennessee and North Carolina. The park is known for its natural scenery and wildlife. The preservation of this natural landscape is due in large part to Anne Davis, who is known as the "Mother of the Park." Davis was one of the first women to serve in the Tennessee State Legislature in 1925. She led the effort to purchase 78,000 acres of land from the Little River Lumber Company. This land eventually became part of the National Park.

Great Smoky Mountains National Park

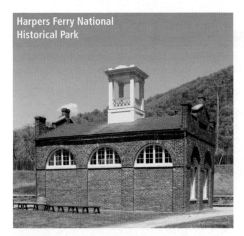
Harpers Ferry National Historical Park

Homestead National Monument of America

Harpers Ferry National Historical Park

This National Historical Park includes parts of West Virginia, Maryland, and Virginia. It is best known for its association with John Brown's raid on the town arsenal in 1859. Though Brown's effort to arm enslaved individuals failed, the fort where he took refuge has become a national symbol. The brick fort was even relocated to Chicago for the 1893 Columbian Exposition. Afterwards, Journalist Kate Field led the effort to move the structure back to its original home in Harpers Ferry.

Harriet Tubman National Historical Park

This National Historical Park is located in Auburn, New York. It tells the story of the famous freedom-seeker and activist Harriet Tubman. Born enslaved, Tubman emancipated herself and led members of her family to freedom in Canada. She and her family eventually settled in Auburn in 1859. Tubman cared for her aging parents and opened her home to other elderly members of the community. She died in 1913 and is buried in Auburn.

Homestead National Monument of America

Located in Nebraska, this National Monument commemorates the Homestead Act of 1862. This law encouraged people to move west and settle on lands being claimed by the US government. The act granted 160 acres of land to applicants, including to women like Rachel Bella Calof. A Jewish immigrant from Russia, Calof and her husband Abraham moved west. They established a homestead near Devils Lake, North Dakota. While there, Rachel helped establish the local school district. She chronicled her adventures in an autobiography.

Joshua Tree National Park

This National Park is located where the Mojave and Colorado Deserts meet in southern California. In the early 1920s, Elizabeth Warder Crozer Campbell and her husband Bill moved to the arid desert terrain for his health. Elizabeth was fascinated by the Native American artifacts and sites near her home. When road construction

Harriet Tubman National Historical Park

Joshua Tree National Park

Knife River Indian Villages
National Historic Site

threatened these places, Elizabeth and other archeologists worked to document them before they were destroyed.

Knife River Indian Villages National Historic Site
This National Historic Site in North Dakota was once the home of Sacagawea. She served as a guide to explorers Lewis and Clark as they traveled west. She is an iconic figure in American history. A Lemhi Shoshone woman originally from what is now Idaho, a young teenage Sacagawea was taken captive. The Hidatsa people who had captured her and others sold her to a French-Canadian fur trader who married her. With her knowledge of the Shoshone language and the land, Meriwether Lewis and William Clark hired her to lead them. She has been celebrated as a symbol of women's independence and strength.

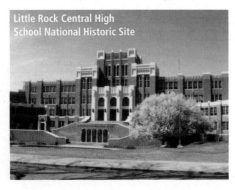
Little Rock Central High School National Historic Site

Little Rock Central High School National Historic Site
This National Historic Site is located in Little Rock, Arkansas. It commemorates the legacy of the nine African American students who integrated the school in 1957. Six of the Little Rock Nine were girls. In 1958, the governor of Arkansas tried to pass legislation that would prevent further integration of the schools. In response, the Women's Emergency Committee was formed. They worked to keep local schools compliant with desegregation laws.

Maggie L. Walker National Historic Site
The home of the first African American woman bank president, this National Historic Site is located in Richmond, Virginia. In 1903 Walker founded the St. Luke Penny Savings Bank and

Maggie L. Walker
National Historic Site

served as its president. She also served her community as an educator, businesswoman, and civil rights activist.

Mary McLeod Bethune Council House National Historic Site

This National Historic Site is located in Washington, DC. It honors the important roles of African American women in social and political movements. Educator and civic leader Mary McLeod Bethune founded the National Council of Negro Women (NCNW) in 1936. The NCNW continues to support organizations around the country that empower Black women and that work for education and economic opportunities in Black communities. The Council House served as the headquarters of the NCNW from 1943 until 1966.

Mount Rainier National Park

This National Park in Washington state is renowned for glaciers and wildflowers as well as its 14,410-foot active volcano. In July 1909, adventurer Dr. Cora Smith Eaton set out to plant a "Votes for Women" flag at the summit of Mount Rainier. She was in the area at the National American Woman Suffrage Association (NAWSA) conference in Seattle. Dr. Eaton was active in

Mount Rainier National Park

Palo Alto Battlefield National Historical Park

both suffrage and mountaineering organizations. Women fighting for voting rights often embarked on physically demanding activities to prove their strength and ability. Unfortunately, the wind was too strong and Dr. Eaton and her team could not reach the summit. Dr. Eaton instead left the flag in one of the mountain craters.

Palo Alto Battlefield National Historical Park

This National Historical Park in Texas preserves the location of the first battle of the Mexican-American War. Women from both countries played important roles during the two-year skirmish. Some women cooked for and aided the soldiers. Some, including Elizabeth Newcome, fought on the battlefield. Women were prohibited from serving in the military, so Newcome disguised herself as a man. For ten months, she served as a private until her identity was discovered.

Rocky Mountain National Park

This National Park in Colorado is famous for its rugged mountain peaks. One person who made the preservation of the park possible was Mary Belle King Sherman. She was an avid clubwoman dedicated to women's involvement in civic life.

Mary McLeod Bethune Council House National Historic Site

Rocky Mountain National Park

ammunition and building trucks, airplanes, and ships. In the park, visitors will find a Rosie the Riveter memorial to all the women who worked at the nearby shipyards to support the war effort.

Statue of Liberty National Monument

A symbol of freedom and democracy, this National Monument is located on Liberty Island in New York City. In 1883, poet Emma Lazarus was asked to write a sonnet for a literary auction. The auction was to raise funds for the statue's pedestal. Lazarus drew on her family's heritage as Jewish immigrants from Portugal, and wrote *The New Colossus*. The poem's most famous line is, "Give me your tired, your poor, your huddled masses yearning to breathe free." It speaks to the importance of Lady Liberty to Americans and those seeking refuge and opportunity here. Lazarus's poem is inscribed on a plaque located on the statue's pedestal.

Sherman became involved in several conservation organizations in the early 1900s. An advocate for the preservation of America's natural landscapes, she played a major role in the founding of Rocky Mountain National Park in 1915.

Rosie the Riveter WWII Home Front National Historical Park

This National Historical Park is located near San Francisco, California. It is dedicated to those who supported the war effort here at home. With many men fighting overseas, American women took over production of supplies. This included producing

Tuskegee Airmen National Historic Site

This National Historic Site in Alabama honors the legacy of the African American pilots who fought in World War II. Discriminatory policies kept Black men out of most pilot programs. Instead, they were sent to Tuskegee University

Rosie the Riveter

Statue of Liberty National Monument

Yellowstone National Park

Yosemite National Park

for training. Women—white or Black—were not permitted to serve in the Air Force. That did not stop Mildred Hemmons Carter from learning to fly. While a student at Tuskegee University, Mildred learned to fly and graduated from the Civilian Pilot Training Program. Unable to serve in World War II as a pilot because of her gender, Carter was hired as a civilian employee with the Army Air Corps. Working there, she directly assisted the Tuskegee program.

Yellowstone National Park

This National Park spans parts of Wyoming, Idaho, and Montana. It is famous for its hydrothermal wonders. Many people (past and present) have been part of the effort to preserve the park. They include Jane Marguerite Lindsley, the first female National Park Service ranger at Yellowstone. Before she began her career as a ranger, Lindsley earned a master's degree in the field of bacteriology. Hired in 1921, she served as a ranger for ten years.

Yosemite National Park

This National Park, located in eastern California, is known for its natural beauty, including waterfalls, valleys, and meadows. The park also has a rich connection to women's history. In the late 1800s, women like Bridget Degnan and Jennie Foster Curry offered goods and services to tourists. Degnan baked and sold bread to tourists while Curry ran a camp at the base of Glacier Point. Others, like the Sweet sisters, sought adventure. In 1896, the sisters and a friend named Mabel Davis became the third group of non-Native American women to climb Mt. Lyell and the first to descend Tuolumne Canyon. As the park became a popular tourist destination, women like Maggie Howard played an important role in preserving and sharing the region's cultural history. A Paiute Indian, Howard spent much of her life in Yosemite Valley. Working at the Yosemite Museum, she performed cultural demonstrations like basket weaving for park visitors.

—Katherine Crawford-Lackey

Tuskegee Airmen National Historic Site

Contributors

Sarah H. Case is continuing lecturer in history at University of California, Santa Barbara. She is the author of *Leaders of Their Race: Educating Black and White Women in the New South* (Illinois, 2017). She is also the managing editor of *The Public Historian*, a journal focused on publicly engaged historical research.

Katherine Crawford-Lackey is a public historian of public commemorations and place-making and history. She is co-editor of the Berghahn Books series on LGBTQ history and historic preservation, *Preservation and Place* (2019), *Identities and Place* (2019), and *Communities and Place* (2020). She received her PhD in public history from Middle Tennessee State University.

Elyssa Ford is an associate professor of history at Northwest Missouri State University where she directs the Honors Program and Public History & Museum Studies Program. She has published in the *Pacific Historical Review, Critical Studies in Men's Fashion, and the Journal of Museum Education*. Her current book project examines race, gender, and cultural identity in American rodeos, and she is completing a project on Alma Nash, a band leader and Missouri participant in the National Woman Suffrage Parade in 1913.

Tamara Gaskell is the director of the Roeliff Jansen Community Library in Hillsdale, NY. She has extensive experience as both a public historian and an editor. She is the assistant editor of the first two volumes of *The Selected Papers of Elizabeth Cady Stanton and Susan B. Anthony* (Rutgers University Press, 1997–2000), was director of publications at the Historical Society of Pennsylvania, and served as co-editor of *The Public Historian* and *The Encyclopedia of Greater Philadelphia*, for which she wrote the essay on woman suffrage.

Liette Gidlow, a specialist in twentieth-century politics and women's and gender history, is the author of *The Big Vote: Gender, Consumer Culture, and the Politics of Exclusion, 1890s–1920s* (Johns Hopkins University Press, 2004), and editor of *Obama, Clinton, Palin: Making History in Election 2008* (University of Illinois Press, 2012). Her next book is a study of the disfranchisement of American women after the Nineteenth Amendment to the Constitution in 1920.

Susan Goodier teaches at SUNY Oneonta and studies US women's activism, particularly woman suffrage activism. She is coordinator for the Upstate New York Women's History Organization and recently edited a double issue on New York State women's suffrage for New York History. She is the author of *No Votes for Women: The New York State Anti-Suffrage Movement* (University of Illinois, 2013) and coauthor of *Women Shall Vote: Winning Suffrage in New York State* (Cornell University Press, 2017). Her current projects include a biography of Louisa M. Jacobs, the daughter of Harriet Jacobs, author of *Incidents in the Life of a Slave Girl* and a history of black women in the New York suffrage movement.

Ann D. Gordon is Research Professor Emerita of History at Rutgers University. She has studied the movement for woman suffrage for nearly four decades as an author, editor, and lecturer. She was chief editor of the prize-winning collection of essays *African American Women and the Vote, 1837–1965* (University of Massachusetts Press, 1997). She also edited the six-volume *Selected Papers of Elizabeth Cady Stanton and Susan B. Anthony* (Rutgers University Press, 1997–2013).

Sharon Harley is associate professor and former chair of the African American Studies Department at the University of Maryland, College Park. She researches and teaches black women's labor history and racial and gender politics. She is coeditor of *The Afro-American Woman: Struggles and Images* (Kennikat Presss, 1978), she edited and contributed essays to *Sister Circle: Black Women and Work* (Rutgers University Press, 2002) and *Women's Labor in the Global Economy: Speaking in Multiple Voices* (Rutgers University Press, 2008).

Jennifer Helton is assistant professor of history at Ohlone College in Fremont, California. Her research focuses on the history of woman suffrage in Wyoming. She contributed a chapter on Wyoming to *Equality at the Ballot Box: Votes for Women on the Northern Great Plains* (South Dakota Historical Society Press, 2019).

Allison K. Lange is an assistant professor of history at the Wentworth Institute of Technology. She is author of *Picturing Political Power: Images in the Women's Suffrage Movement* (University of Chicago, 2020). She is also guest curating suffrage exhibitions at the Massachusetts Historical Society and Harvard's Schlesinger Library.

Robyn Muncy is professor of history at the University of Maryland, College Park. She is author of *Creating a Female Dominion in American Reform, 1890–1935* (Oxford, 1991) and *Relentless Reformer: Josephine Roche and Progressivism in Twentieth-Century America* (Princeton, 2015). She is guest curator of *Rightfully Hers: American Women and the Vote*, an exhibit to commemorate the centenary of the ratification of the Nineteenth Amendment at the National Archives in Washington, DC (March 2019–September 2020).

Heather Munro Prescott is professor of history at Central Connecticut State University. Her research and teaching interests include US women's history, history of medicine and public health, and the history of childhood and youth. Her first book, *A Doctor of Their Own: The History of Adolescent Medicine* (Harvard, 1998), received the Will Solimene Award of Excellence in Medical Communication from the New England Chapter, American Medical Writers Association. Her most recent book is *The Morning After: A History of Emergency Contraception in the United States* (Rutgers, 2011).

Christine L. Ridarsky is historian for the City of Rochester, New York, and historical services consultant for the Central Library of Rochester & Monroe County, where she manages the Local History & Genealogy Division. She has an MA in American history from the State University Of New York, College at Brockport, and is ABD toward a PhD in American history at the University of Rochester. She is co-editor of *Susan B. Anthony and the Struggle for Equal Rights* (University of Rochester Press, 2012) and editor of the journal, *Rochester History*.

Rebecca A. Rix is an independent scholar of US gender, political and legal history, whose research focuses on the changing nature of the franchise in the history of American republicanism. She earned her PhD in history from Yale University in 2008 and held an assistant professorship in history at Princeton University, 2009–17. Her current book project analyzes anti-suffragism to illuminate the transformation of republicanism from a family-based to an individual-based model between Reconstruction and the New Deal.

Judith Wellman is professor emerita, State University of New York at Oswego, and director, Historical New York Research Associates. She specializes in historic sites relating to women's rights, the Underground Railroad, and African American life. She is the author of several books and articles, including *The Road to Seneca Falls: Elizabeth Cady Stanton and the First Woman's Rights Convention* (University of Illinois Press, 2004).

Cover Special Collections and Archives, VCU Libraries

Back Cover Mary B. Talbert, ca. 1901, courtesy of the Collection of the Buffalo History Museum, Buffalo, NY

Title Page and Inside Front Cover Courtesy of Virginia Museum of History & Culture, http://www.VirginiaHistory.com

Contents Page National Woman's Party Records, I:160, Library of Congress

4 Library of Congress, P&P, LC-USZ62-5664

6 National Park Service photographs, Library of Congress, P&P, LC-DIG-ppmsca-38385

7 Library of Congress, P&P, LC-DIG-ppmsca-39001, LC-DIG-ppmsca-58145

8 Library of Congress, P&P, LC-USZ62-95372, LC-DIG-hec-02086

9 Library of Congress, P&P, LC-USZ62-107756, LC-DIG-ppmsca-53150

10 Library of Congress, P&P, LC-H261-6590

11 Library of Congress, P&P, LC-USZ62-66358

12 National Park Service photograph

13 National Park Service photograph

17 Courtesy of the John W. Carr/Vineland Historical and Antiquarian Society, Vineland, NJ

18 Detail from engraving by John Chester Buttre, ca. 1882, made for *History of Woman Suffrage*, volume 2

20 *Harper's Weekly*, November 24, 1894, 1124

24 Library of Congress, P&P, LC-DIG-ggbain-34493

26 Photograph by Laura Shea. Courtesy Mount Holyoke College Art Museum, South Hadley, Massachusetts (2015.9)

27 Courtesy of the Schomburg Center for Research in Black Culture, Photographs and Prints Division, The New York Public Library

30 Library of Congress, P&P, LC-DIG-ppmsca-40924

32 Library of Congress, Manuscript Division, National Woman's Party Records (11:275)

35 Library of Congress, P&P, LC-DIG-ggbain-18817

37 Courtesy of the Library of Virginia, Richmond

38 Courtesy Carrie Chapman Catt Papers, Special Collections Department, Bryn Mawr College Library, Bryn Mawr, PA

44 Courtesy Carrie Chapman Catt Albums, part of the Carrie Chapman Catt Papers at Bryn Mawr College Library Special Collections Department, Bryn Mawr, PA

46 Courtesy Carrie Chapman Catt Albums, part of the Carrie Chapman Catt Papers at Bryn Mawr College Library Special Collections, Bryn Mawr, PA

48 Library of Congress, MSS, LC-USZ62-31799

51 Library of Congress, P&P, LC-DIG-pga-13043

53 Library of Congress, P&P, LC-DIG-pga-04866

56 Miller NAWSA Suffrage Scrapbooks, 1897–1911, Library of Congress

58 Courtesy of the author

59 Miller NAWSA Suffrage Scrapbooks, 1897–1911, Library of Congress

63 NPS photos

65 Frontspiece, *Poems* by Frances E. W. Harper. George S. Ferguson Co., 1898. Library of Congress, LC-USZ62-118946

68 Library of Congress, P&P, LC-USZ62-54722

70 From *The Afro-American Press and its Editors* by I. Garland Penn, 1891. Library of Congress LC-USZ62-107756

71 Courtesy of the Collection of the Buffalo History Museum, Buffalo, NY

73 Library of Congress, P&P, LC-USZ62-79903

75 Courtesy, American Antiquarian Society

77 Library of Congress, P&P, LC-DIG-ppmsca-08978

78 Library of Congress, P&P, LC-USZ62-5664

80 From *Puck*, February 20, 1915. Library of Congress, P&P, LC-DIG-ppmsca-40504

85 Courtesy of Bryn Mawr College Library Special Collections, Bryn Mawr, PA

89 Courtesy of L.Tom Perry Special Collections, Harold B. Lee Library, Brigham Young University, Provo, UT

90 Courtesy of the Western History Photographic Collections F45641, Denver Public Library

91 Courtesy of Women's Suffrage and Equal Rights Collection, Ella Strong Denison Library, Scripps College, Claremont, CA

93 Courtesy of Women's Suffrage and Equal Rights Collection, Ella Strong Denison Library, Scripps College, Claremont, CA

95 Courtesy of Bergere Family Photograph Collection, Image #21702, New Mexico State Records Center and Archives, Santa Fe, NM

97 Library of Congress, P&P, LC-DIG-highsm-43402, Library of Congress, P&P, LC-USF346-052166-D

98 From *The Oregonian Souvenir*, Lewis and Dryden 1892; by Daderot, CC 1.0 Public Domain, Wikimedia Commons; Library of Congress, P&P, LC-USZ62-55735

99 Library of Congress, P&P, LC-USZ62-56632, Library of Congress, P&P, LC-USZ62-82848

101 Library of Congress, MSS, National Woman's Party Records I: 160

105 *Broad Ax* (Chicago, IL), November 15, 1913

106 Library of Congress, P&P, LC-USZ62-30776

109 Miller NAWSA Suffrage Scrapbooks, 1897-1911, Library of Congress

111 Courtesy of the Missouri Historical Society, St. Louis

113 Library of Congress, P&P, LC-USZ62-77001

116 National Woman's Party Records, 1:150, Library of Congress

118 National Woman's Party Records, II:275, Library of Congress

119 National Woman's Party Records, I:160, Library of Congress

122 National Woman's Party Records, II:275

123 From *The Life and Work of Susan B. Anthony* by Ida Husted Harper, Bowen-Merrill Co., 1899, Library of Congress

124 From *The History of Woman Suffrage*, Vol. 3 by Stanton et al.

126 Courtesy of the Local History & Genealogy Division, Rochester (NY) Public Library

127 From the *Authentic History of the Douglass Monument*, Rochester Herald Press, 1903

128 National Woman's Party Records, 1:155, Library of Congress

131 National Woman's Party Records, I:157, Library of Congress

133 Carol Highsmith, Library of Congress, P&P, LC-DIG-highsm-28801

136 Courtesy of Virginia Museum of History & Culture, http://www.VirginiaHistory.com

137 National Woman's Party Records, 1:151, Library of Congress

139 Library of Congress, P&P, LC-USZ62-54722

142 Courtesy of the Schlesinger Library, Radcliffe Institute, Harvard University, Cambridge, MA; *The Suffragist*, March 24, 1917, courtesy of Belmont-Paul Women's Equality National Monument, home of the historic National Woman's Party, Washington, DC

143 George and Edna Rapuzzi Collection, Rasmuson Foundation, Klondike Gold Rush National Historical Park, print inventory #000147

145 National Park Service photograph

147 Courtesy of Charles Lenhart

149 Courtesy of the Alice Paul Institute

150 Courtesy of Carrie Chapman Catt Girlhood Home and Museum; Courtesy of Judith Wellman

152 National Park Service photograph

158 Photo AR.E.004 (028), Austin History Center, Austin (TX) Public Library, published with permission

160 Grand Rapids Americanization Society, ca. 1924, from the collections of the Smithsonian National Museum of American History

163 Courtesy of the Virginia State University Special Collections and Archives, used with permission

166-173 National Park Service photographs; by Carol Highsmith, Library of Congress, P&P, LC-DIG-highsm-13326, LC-DIG-highsm-31333, LC-DIG-highsm-23456; Library of Congress, P&P, HABS DC, WASH, 589-34 (CT); by Pwsuddess, CC BY-SA 4.0, Wikimedia Commons.

Notes:
MSS = Manuscript Collection
P&P = Prints & Photographs Division